# BIBLICAL THEMES FOR PASTORAL CARE

# BIBLICAL THEMES FOR PASTORAL CARE

## WILLIAM B. OGLESBY JR.

Abingdon Press
Nashville

BIBLICAL THEMES FOR PASTORAL CARE

*Copyright © 1980 by William B. Oglesby, Jr.*

*This book is printed on recycled, acid-free paper.*

**Library of Congress Cataloging-in-Publication Data**

OGLESBY, WILLIAM B.
   Biblical themes for pastoral care.
   1. Pastoral counseling. 2. Bible—Use. I. Title.
   BV4012.2.034        253.5        79-26828

**ISBN 0-687-03447-7**

96 97 98 99 00 01 02 03—15 14 13 12

MANUFACTURED IN THE UNITED STATES OF AMERICA

# Contents

# Preface

Does the Bible have anything to say to the minister who engages in the task of pastoral counseling? And if so, what?

For many in our day, these questions are not really relevant. For whatever reason, they have reached the conclusion that the Bible, however it may relate to devotional pursuits and personal edification, really has little if anything to do with the practical functioning of the minister. On the other hand, there are those who believe that the Bible provides a kind of "book of rules" that may be applied to any situation on virtually a one-to-one basis, giving answers to questions raised by troubled persons, providing guideposts for the solution of problems, and equipping the pastor with a kind of manual to which s/he can turn for authoritative directives for his/her parishioners.[1]

Perhaps the vast majority of ministers fall somewhere in between these two positions. They reject any sort of "code of conduct" notion of the Bible and yet feel that there is, or should be, relevance in the ancient documents for contemporary living. But how to discover the relevance, they aren't sure.

It is with these various attitudes in mind that I write this book. It may be that those who consider the Bible irrelevant will not be greatly changed in their point of view, if, indeed, they ever read these pages. It is even less likely that those who consider the Bible as a set of rules will give up such a notion, since it provides a rather painless way to encounter the ambiguities of life. Thus, it is to the persons who in one form or other do find themselves in the position in between that I am writing.

My interest in this undertaking has emerged from many sources. While in any technical sense mine is not the biblical field, the study of the Bible has been for me a lifelong interest beginning in early childhood as we heard before bedtime selections from Hurlbut's *Story of the Bible*. Those early impressions are still with me, although my notions regarding the "heroes" of the Bible underwent realistic changes as I learned to read the text on my own, uncensored by well-meaning Bible storytellers. It was then that I discovered something of the profound meaning in the fact that these people were of "like passions as we" (James 5:17 KJV) and became aware that their story is our story.

Against this background, the task of teaching pastoral counseling to theological students in a seminary of the Reformed tradition meant that I had to take seriously the implications of the biblical revelation for the work of the minister. It was one thing to resist the devotional or moralistic tendency of books on the relationship between the Bible and pastoral care. It was something else to formulate an alternative approach that would take into account the nature of the biblical material and studies in the behavioral sciences. For me, the process took shape slowly. As will be evident to my former students who read these words, my own position has developed through the years, a process that is still continuing. As I think back, there were several major factors that helped shape the course of my explorations.

My thinking was greatly stimulated by the renewal in biblical studies after World War II in what has been called the era of biblical theology. I was drawn by the stress on the use of the Bible in ministry even though most of the emphasis was on preaching and teaching rather than pastoral care. It was during this same time that my work with alcoholics taught me the futility of most of the strategies we had assumed were appropriate for helping persons in difficulty. As a result of these experiences, I realized that advice, however valid in itself, was practically useless in terms of any long-range transformation. In like manner, it became clear to me that appealing to logic as a means for resolving the issues and problems of life was equally nonproductive. In reflecting on these lessons so dearly learned from the suffering of others, I came to understand in a new light the meaning of justification by grace through faith. In 1950 I went to the University of Chicago, and during the following two years my association with Carl Rogers helped me appreciate the importance of empathic relationships particularly in terms of the freeing effect on the person which came in an experience of acceptance. There were, of course, other factors; but these stand out in my memory as primary, and in the chapters that follow they are discussed in great detail.

In 1966 I put together my thinking thus far in *With Wings as Eagles* (Richmond: CLC Press; 2nd ed., Abingdon, 1979), which is a semi-novel based on the story of the Elder Brother and the Prodigal as a means for understanding growth and maturity. Here, I drew on biblical material not only for the basic theme of the book but to indicate how the Bible is related to all manner of circumstances in the changing conditions of life. There are in the book various incidents of pastoral care and counseling; but because of its primary purpose, only scant attention is given to discussing the biblical basis for the principles inherent in these situations.

It was shortly thereafter, in continued reflection on these matters, that the idea of exploring various facets or themes of the biblical material began to take form. These concepts have been discussed with wide varieties of persons, and I have greatly profited by the depth of understanding that these discussions represented. I think of lay groups in local congregations, of ministers' conferences, of formal classes in an academic setting, and I am grateful to all those who have served to challenge and sharpen my own understanding. It is likely that readers may find notions here that they recognize as having roots in some suggestion or comment that they made in such a discussion. I would like to give particular appreciation for all such, although by now the whole has developed in my own thinking so as to blur the source of the many individual contributions. But to all those who helped in this fashion, may I say that these words would never have appeared if it had not been for you. Not all of you will agree with what I have written, just as you did not agree when we discussed the material! No matter. I was as much helped by disagreement as agreement, and I would like to express my sincere appreciation to each of you and all of you together.

The writing has gone slowly. Begun in Rüschlikon, Switzerland, in 1974, there have been revisions and additions in an attempt to make the material as relevant and clear as possible. These are times of foment in pastoral care. The creative emphasis on family therapy, the renewed understanding of the corporate nature of ministry, the emergence of concern for spiritual dimensions of life all make for an exciting context in which the work of the pastor is to be accomplished. The fact is that anything written tends to become dated before it can be published. The time finally came when I realized that if I waited until there was some sort of stable concensus regarding the work of the ministry the book would never be done. Therefore, I decided to strike the. final period, even though in doing so I am aware of the continued movement of my own progression in the matter of pastoral care.

Thus, it is my hope that the ideas set forth here will serve two purposes. In the first place, I am convinced that a responsible use of the Bible is basic in the performance of constructive pastoral counseling and can provide needed principles whereby the minister may evaluate ongoing pastoral work and make constructive use of data that have emerged from the behavioral sciences. And in the second place, I trust that the concepts I describe and illustrate will be a stimulus to many to press for further clarification and elucidation so that all of us who attempt to be faithful to our calling as ministers of the Word may have a clearer understanding of the means whereby we fulfill our function as pastoral counselors.

Earlier I expressed appreciation for all those persons who, as my ideas were being formulated, stimulated and enriched my continued exploration of the implications for *Biblical Themes for Pastoral Care*. Here I would like to say a particular word of thanks to Sandra Brown of Princeton Theological Seminary for helpful suggestions and for making available some of the case material. In like fashion, my colleague on the faculty of Union Seminary, Professor Sibley Towner, did me the favor of reading the material from the perspective of a biblical scholar, and his comments steered me through many critical areas of interpretation. Since I did not always follow the suggestions of these friends, the material as presented is my responsibility, not theirs. To Sally Hicks and Joy Heebink I am indebted for the typing of the final manuscript, and, as scholars in their own right, providing helpful comments on content and format.

One final word about the format of the book. The first chapter is crucial for all that follows since it contains my understanding of the principles that emerge from biblical material as they relate to pastoral care. The subsequent chapters are illustrative, using case material to show how the biblical data are translated into actual procedure. For this reason, I hope that the reader will follow the argument in the first chapter as closely as possible whether in agreement or disagreement in order to understand the basis for the more detailed analyses that appear as each biblical theme is explored in relation to process in pastoral counseling.

> Rüschlikon, Switzerland
> Spring, 1974
>
> Richmond, Virginia
> Fall, 1979

[1]The problems with language, particularly the third person singular pronouns and the generic terms for persons, continue to plague us. I look forward to the day when we will have adopted a less cumbersome style than is now available. In the second edition of my *Referral in Pastoral Counseling* (Abingdon, 1978), I set forth a proposal for some such terms as "se" for "he/she," "hir" for "him/her," and "hes" for "his/her." I still believe such a form is possible, but am pessimistic about our agreement on this or any similar proposal in the near future. Therefore, in this book I will use "s/he" for "he/she," "wo/man" for "man/woman," and the usual "his/her" and "him/her," all the while looking forward to a better day.

# Chapter One

## The Bible and Pastoral Care and Counseling

To speak of the "Bible" and "pastoral care and counseling" is not to speak in a vacuum. There is little likelihood that anyone who reads these pages will not already have a fairly well-formed notion of what is essentially meant by each of these terms, even if the notion is more impressionistic than carefully thought out. For this reason, anyone who attempts to write about either can be certain that the reader is moving from personal presuppositions that are not necessarily those of the author; and the task is compounded when two such widely used terms are brought together. This is in no sense to deplore such presuppositions. It is to say that in my task of dealing with the issues I am aware of the varieties of presuppositions and definitions and have attempted to keep them in mind in the presentation of the material so that there can be some sense of dialogue between the reader and me.

With that in mind, the purpose of this chapter is to discuss the observable relationship between the Bible and pastoral care and counseling as illustrated in several brief verbatim excerpts, and then to comment on these from the perspective of the biblical message as a whole. This leads us to an exploration of the sense in which the Bible is involved not only with theory but also with practice in the work of the minister, that is, the way the

Bible informs not only what the minister believes but also how s/he actually relates to persons in pastoral situations.[1]

On the basis of this exploration, I set forth several motifs or themes that enable the minister to determine the kind of process in pastoral care and counseling that is consistent with the biblical material. Finally, there is an overall view of the format followed in the succeeding chapters with some explanation of the use of case material to illustrate the principles drawn from biblical data.

# I

It goes without saying that the importance of pastoral care and counseling has been recognized by the church from the beginning. Bearing one another's burdens and so fulfilling the law of Christ (Gal. 6:2) is a responsibility entrusted to every member of the family of faith, but is specifically charged to the minister as the "shepherd of the flock," to use a traditional metaphor. No one doubts *that* it should be done. The crucial question turns on *how* it should be done, and this is the question that we address here.[2]

Through the years there have been varieties of fashions that have been employed in an attempt to be faithful in pastoral care. John T. McNeill's *History of the Cure of Souls* documents the often antithetical practices that have marked this ministry.[3] The focus has turned from support to scourge and back again as the church has dealt with troubled and penitent persons. Practically any practice today can find some precedent in history, and it should not surprise us that there is such an unevenness in our time.

More recently the process of pastoral care and

counseling has drawn on the researches and experiences of the behavioral sciences. This has been a very positive gain as we have been instructed by those who have devoted their lives to helping persons in distress. Many ministers now use the terminology of the psychotherapies with understanding and skill, speaking of compulsions, hysteria, depression, projection, and the like. The literature of psychotherapy is read alongside the literature on theology, and there are probably not too many clergy who are unacquainted with "Psychoanalysis," "T.A.," "Client-Centered Therapy," "Reality Therapy," "Gestalt," and a host of others even if the basic presuppositions of each are not clearly grasped.

The question, then, becomes, How is the minister to utilize these genuine advances, and what criteria are available to enable the minister to make a discriminating judgment in regard to the values and disvalues in each? More specifically, in terms of our focus in this discussion, does the Bible shed any light on the matter so that the minister may have a responsible means for ordering the process of pastoral care?

To prevent our staying entirely in abstract concepts, I give three brief examples to help identify the presuppositions that lie behind most if not all practices in pastoral care and counseling. Imagine a man in his mid-thirties who seeks the aid of his minister in regard to some personal matter that is bothering him. Each minister, for the sake of the illustration, is a person who cares about the parishioner and is genuinely desirous of helping. It is likely that if this parishioner were to go to three ministers he would hear different responses based not simply on the fact that all persons are different but also on the different concept each minister has as to what is essentially helpful.

Minister A listens to the parishioner state his problem and then says, in effect: "I'm glad you've come, although I regret the circumstance that has brought you here. I certainly want to be of help if I can. Perhaps you and I can explore the meaning and implications of what is happening to you and gain a clearer understanding of what has led up to now and what can be done about it." If the parishioner went to Minister B, he might hear, in effect, the first sentence, and then: "Perhaps we can explore more effective ways to respond to the issues and situations you face so that you won't continually be working yourself into a corner." Minister C would doubtless indicate a genuine willingness to help and then continue: "You've really had a rough time, and right now you're caught in a bind, not sure just which way to go."

If pressed for a rationale or purpose undergirding the intent of each statement, the ministers would respond in somewhat different ways. Minister A might say, "I see this person as someone who is unaware of the meaning of his behavior, and I hope to help him gain a more perceptive understanding of the various factors involved so that he may live more creatively." Minister B, on the other hand, might answer, "As I see it, he has been and is being defeated by the way he reacts to various situations, and I hope he can be motivated to find more constructive ways of doing things and thus not get caught in so many painful consequences." In still another vein, Minister C might say: "I see him as one who is hurt and bewildered and I hope to relate to him in such a way that he will begin to experience creativity and freedom in the context of trust."

In general terms, Minister A believes that if the parishioner can gain some insight into his situation, he will be better able to deal with the dynamics and ambiguities that heretofore have tended to defeat him. Minister B hopes that when the parishioner begins to act in different and more constructive ways his life will be more satisfying and productive. Finally, Minister C is convinced that what is most helpful is a renewal of broken relationships, and that, in an experience of understanding and acceptance, the parishioner will no longer be bound by distortions of thought and behavior that cause frustration and pain.

It is evident, of course, that each minister has been influenced, either consciously or unconsciously, by the primary emphases of therapy in our culture. Minister A draws on insight-oriented therapy in the expectation that when the person knows more constructively what the often hidden and inner dynamics of his/her life are, then s/he will be able to structure the processes of living in a more creative fashion. By the same token, Minister B has been influenced by behaviorism, and is convinced that if the parishioner can be motivated to act in a different fashion, his/her confusion will tend to dissipate and his/her inner tension will be reduced. Finally, Minister C does not believe that either right knowing or right doing will be effective as a means for resolving the issues of life. Influenced by the relationship-oriented therapies, s/he is convinced that in the encounter of the counseling experience the parishioner is set free from the debilitating patterns of behavior and is able to discern meaning in life that has hitherto been obscure.

Although these three illustrations are presented in the barest of sketches, the underlying presuppositions of the ministers are nonetheless relevant to the task of ministry. It is evident that all three are genuinely concerned with right knowing (insight or self-understanding), right doing (behavior modification), and right being (personal transformation). The critical factor is, which of these emphases is seen as primary, from which the other two derive. The first believes that if the parishioner can gain insight into his situation he will act more responsibly and thus relate to others more effectively. The second is convinced that if s/he can assist in motivating the parishioner to act differently, his perceptions and relationships will be enhanced. Finally, the third minister sees the relationships as primary, and if broken relationships can be reestablished, then the perceptions and actions will improve.

It can be argued that the question of focus turns not so much on principle as on the situation of the person, that one approach is better for this person while another is better for that. So, the argument goes, since all three are important and all three are always present, it is not a matter of moment where one initially concentrates the counseling experience. Such an argument, however, tends to obscure the fundamental presuppositions regarding what constitutes help for the person in trouble. In psychoanalysis, for example, the transference is essential, but only as a means for effecting the relationship that can make the basic focus, i.e., understanding, possible. Likewise, a focus on behavior may, and often does, presuppose a good rapport between the counselor and the parishioner. Here, also, the rapport is seen as that which is an avenue toward accomplishing the real purpose, i.e., alteration of behavior. A primary focus on relationship, however, does not view the experience of encounter as a means to a more significant end; rather it is seen as an end in itself, although as noted above, better knowing and doing will emerge from better being.

## II

We turn now to a consideration of what guidance may be discovered in the Bible to inform the minister's presuppositions and practice in pastoral care. Our purpose here is to explore the sense in which biblical material provides guidelines and criteria not only for what the minister believes but also for what s/he does in pastoral care.[4]

### A

As I write these words I can recall reading literally hundreds of verbatim accounts prepared by students in the seminary and ministers in parish and specialized settings. As a teacher of pastoral care and counseling my purpose has been to enable the students and ministers to examine the verbatim as the unit of pastoral care in the context of the dynamics of the relationship between the parishioner and persons in his/her life and, more specifically, between the parishioner and the minister. Each student or minister has an opportunity to reflect on what happened in the pastoral conversation and whether s/he did that which now in retrospect seems constructive or destructive. As the discussion moves forward, criteria for evaluative comments tend to be pragmatic ("this seemed to turn out all right," or "this did not seem to be very effective") or imitational ("this is the way my teacher does it," or "my reading has been in 'X' theory and that makes sense to me.") Only rarely are biblical data adduced as a basis for evaluation and revision.[5]

The reasons for this fact are in some sense understandable. There are those who are not particularly convinced that the Bible is the place to look for pastoral process. After all, they reason, the Bible is an ancient book, useful for devotional and ethical matters, but hardly relevant to the matter of theory and practice of pastoral care and counseling. Others hold that the Bible is normative for personal faith and life, but do not perceive its direct relevance for evaluating verbatim case material. My own Presbyterian tradition has firm roots in biblical authority as attested by the confessional documents that see the Scriptures of the Old and New Testaments as "the only infallible rule of faith and practice," principally teaching "what man is to believe concerning God and what duty God requires of man."[6] However doctrinally clear these statements are, any minister, Presbyterian or not, who has attempted to translate them into the conducting of a counseling conversation can attest that the translation is complex indeed.

The fact, of course, is that the Bible was not written to provide a manual or book of rules for everything the minister does. There is no chapter devoted to the preparation and delivery of sermons, or to effective methods for teaching preschool children, or to strategies for successful pastoral care and counseling. Thus, any understanding of the implication of biblical material for ministerial function comes from an interpretation of Scripture rather than from a how-to-do-it pericope. Since interpretation is subject to varieties of opinion, the pastor is often uncertain just how to relate the Bible to pastoral care and counseling by translating the notion of "rule of faith and practice" into actual procedure. The plain fact is that such a translation is scarcely ever attempted at all.

This does not mean that the students and ministers who presented the verbatims were unconcerned with the Bible. Quite the contrary. And if, as often happened in the seminars where I was a participant, they were pressed a bit for some biblical rationale for their approach they would ordinarily take the matter seriously and, in the ensuing discussion, point to one or more biblical texts or pericopes which, as they saw it, provided support for their pastoral interventions. Those whose verbatims followed the focus of Minister A in the illustrations given above might cite some such text as John 8:32—"And you will know the truth, and the truth will make you free"—or perhaps the account of Jesus' conversation with the woman of Sychar. In the latter, the point being made was that Jesus moved skillfully toward enabling the woman to explore the inner meaning of her life and attitude toward a more effective coping with day-to-day experience. The verse generally noted as evidence of the effectiveness of this strategy is John 4:29, where the woman is reported as saying to her friends in the city, "Come, see a man who told me all that I ever did." There are, of course, countless others, but these illustrate both the use of a text and a narrative as the basis for moving toward understanding and insight.

By the same token, those who responded in the perspective of Minister B often found support in such texts as I Timothy 6:2—"Teach and urge these duties"— an instruction of Paul to the young pastor which appeared to suggest a more behavioristic approach. In regard to narrative pericopes the list is lengthy. Most often cited was the encounter between Jesus and the rich young ruler, noting specifically: "One thing you still lack. Sell all that you have and distribute to the poor, and you will have treasure in heaven; and come, follow me" (Luke 18:22; cf. also Matt. 19:21 and Mark 10:21). Others, as would be expected, include the conversation with the lawyer in Luke 10 leading to the story of the good Samaritan, the instructions to the lepers in Luke 17, and many more.

Finally, those who took the approach of Minister C

found that turning to a text or narrative pericope did not seem quite as possible as was the case for Minister A and even more so for Minister B. However, some suggested Ephesians 2:14, 15: "For he is our peace, who has made us both one, and has broken down the dividing wall of hostility . . . and might reconcile us both to God in one body," or Romans 3:23-25: "since all have sinned and fall short of the glory of God, they are justified by his grace as a gift . . . to be received by faith." In terms of a pericope, a similar difficulty appeared. Some cited the healing of the lame man at the pool of Bethzatha as recorded in John 5, although they were not certain about the relationship between Jesus and the man. Still others thought that the story of the two brothers in Luke 15 exemplified the basic principle of restoration and reconciliation apart from emphasis on right knowing or right doing.

It is evident in each instance that the persons who believed their primary focus was the most appropriate could turn to the Bible and find support for their position. The fact that this was true for all three groups led to the awareness that more was needed than such citations, an awareness that is, in and of itself, quite essential to any responsible use of the Bible as a criterion for the practice of pastoral care and counseling. In light of this understanding, we turn now to a consideration of those factors which are helpful in assessing the biblical implications for pastoral care.

In the first place, it is certain that appeal to this or that text for deriving a basis for any or all strategies in the work of ministry is fraught with danger from the beginning. The obvious problem with this sort of proof-text use of Scripture is that it fails to take into account the intent of the passage and the context in which it is set. Whether the text be used to support the pressing for insight, the prescribing or pressing for change in behavior, or the restoration of personal relationships, the basic distortion is the same. Through the years some of the darkest hours of the church have been marked by using a text to support some previously derived notion or idea. The resistance to the Copernican hypothesis on the basis of Psalm 96 ("The earth is established and cannot be moved") or the harassment and killing of women in the Salem "witch hunts" on the grounds of Exodus 22:18 ("Thou shalt not suffer a witch to live"—KJV) are stark illustrations of ways in which biblical words have been employed to provide a rationale for that which was being undertaken, however sincerely. It is regrettable that ministers who would and do decry such practices unwittingly or inadvertently fall into the same trap in regard to pastoral care and counseling. This is not to say that the texts are unimportant or should be ignored. On the contrary, they need to be taken quite seriously. But it is precisely the taking of them seriously that requires that we look beyond the immediate verse or verses for the basic meaning of the passage.

The same kind of caveat is appropriate to the use of the narrative pericopes. The fact is that these stories are not intended to be used as models for practice in pastoral care.[7] They are not set forth as verbatims in our present understanding of that term, and to require them to answer the question, How do I actually respond in a pastoral conversation? is to move away from their essential meaning and intention. The fact is that the Bible was not written to answer any and all questions we might bring to it. On the contrary, the Bible sits in judgment on the questions, and to an incorrectly asked question there can be no correct answer.[8] Only when we take quite seriously the Bible's inherent purpose at any given point can we move with appropriate conviction regarding what it is we are to do in the work of ministry.

This is not to say that the narrative passages of Scripture have no significance for the work of the minister. On the contrary, as in the case of a text or pericope, they contain valuable data, but these data are useful only when understood on the basis of their essential structure and meaning. When read not as verbatims designed to give clues for procedure, but as material designed to enable us to understand the meaning of God's redemption as supremely set forth in the life, death, and resurrection of Jesus, these narratives are rich in providing the minister with a foundation upon which to base any and all pastoral encounters. Just how this is realized is discussed in greater detail after we have explored the biblical principles which enable us to discern between the three approaches with which we have been dealing.

### B

Having looked at the inappropriateness of utilizing a text or narrative pericope uncritically as the basis for deriving procedure in pastoral care and counseling, we turn now to a consideration of the sense in which the Bible provides help in wrestling with the issue posed by the varying presuppositions underlying the practice of Ministers A, B, and C. As has been noted, the basic notion informing the practice of Minister A is that knowledge is curative, and if s/he can enable the person to gain some understanding of the inner dynamics of the situation then it is possible to work out a more constructive way to life. Minister B, on the other hand, is influenced by behavior modification principles and believes that if, by reward or punishment, it is possible to alter the person's way of responding then life will be more open and satisfying. By contrast, Minister C draws on relationship therapies in the conviction that as distorted relationships are overcome by an encounter marked by realistic trust and genuine openness, the person's perceptions and actions will become more fulfilling.

It is evident that the Bible sees all three concepts as important. Indeed, there is a sense in which the whole story of God's revelation and human response can be told in terms of "knowing," "doing," and "being."[9] The crucial question, as suggested above, is which of these is seen as primary and which derivative.

In regard to "knowing," one has but to consult a concordance to discover its relevance in both the Old Testament and the New. An investigation of the passages, however, reveals a significant factor. Knowing, in the sense of grasping conceptual matters concerning human behavior or the world, is perceived as of relatively secondary importance. The notion of "know thyself," so familiar to us from Greek philosophy and so much a part of our efforts in self-understanding, is singularly absent. Throughout, the knowing that is important is the knowledge of God. In Exodus 33:13, Moses prays, "Show me now thy ways, that I may know thee," and Jeremiah in speaking of the new covenant looks for the day when "they shall all know me, from the least of them to the greatest, says the Lord" (31:34).

In the same vein, Job clearly distinguishes between the knowledge of God and all other knowledge. The futility of the latter is seen in such passages as 6:28 ff; 9:1 ff; and 12:2 ff; the primary significance of the former is found in his two basic affirmations: "I know that my Redeemer lives" (19:25), and "I know that thou canst do all things" (42:2). The Eden story suggests that knowledge in and of

25

itself is destructive (Gen. 3:22), and the writer of Ecclesiastes sees wisdom as an "unhappy business" so that "he who increaseth knowledge increases sorrow" (1:18). This is not to say that wisdom is wrong. As Ecclesiastes reminds us, "wisdom excels folly as light excels darkness" (2:13). However, in the long run it makes little difference in and of itself. "One fate comes to all" (2:14). The essential point is that knowledge for its own sake is futile in the long run.

The importance of the knowledge of God is everywhere evident in the New Testament. Jesus, in the garden prayer, says: "This is eternal life, that they know thee the only true God, and Jesus Christ whom thou hast sent" (John 17:3). This theme is recurrent in the writings of Paul, e.g., "that I may know him and the power of his resurrection" (Phil. 3:10), and "I know whom I have believed" (II Tim. 1:12). Moreover, there is a cryptic and disturbing reference to the possible danger of knowledge in and of itself in II Peter 2:21: "For it would have been better for them never to have known the way of righteousness than after knowing it to turn back."

This does not mean that there is no self-understanding or self-awareness as such in the Bible. On the contrary, such occurs often. But it comes not as a consequence of self-examination but in response to an encounter with God. And it leads not to release and newness of life, it leads to despair. We hear this in Isaiah's lament: "Woe is me! For I am lost; for I am a man of unclean lips . . . ; for my eyes have seen the King, the Lord of hosts!" (6:5). The same awareness is echoed in Simon Peter's "Depart from me, for I am a sinful man, O Lord" (Luke 5:8) as a consequence of his encounter with Jesus.

Many additional references are available, but the point is clear. "Knowing" in human experience regarding the self is derivative rather than primary. Self-knowledge and the knowledge of God come not as a consequence of "searching out" through cognitive striving, but in the response of faith as trust—*fiducia*—as we encounter God.[10] It is certain that Jesus emphasized teaching in his own ministry and in the ministry and lives of his disciples. Nevertheless, the unique symbol of the new life is the cross, not the dialogue; indeed, it is the cross that makes the dialogue possible.

In regard to "doing," the Bible everywhere attests to its importance, as we have seen is true in regard to "knowing." The Decalogue, together with the varieties of codes and regulations, gives evidence that human action and behavior are taken exceedingly seriously. The blessings and punishments for right and wrong doing occur over and over. Illustrative are passages in Deuteronomy 6: "You shall not go after other gods . . . lest the anger of the Lord your God be kindled against you" (14, 15); "you shall do what is right and good in the sight of the Lord, that it may go well with you" (18); "it will be righteousness for us, if we are careful to do all this commandment" (25).[11]

In the New Testament, as well, there is continued the importance of right doing. The Sermon on the Mount concludes with Jesus' solemn warning: "Not every one who says to me, 'Lord, Lord,' shall enter the kingdom of heaven, but he who does the will of my Father who is in heaven. . . . 'Depart from me, you evildoers' " (Matt. 7:21, 23). Likewise in many parables, appropriate action is praised, e.g., in the statement of the nobleman to the servant: "Well done, good servant! Because you have been faithful in a very little, you shall have authority over ten cities" (Luke 19:17; cf. also Matt. 25:14 ff). Other illustrations abound in which persons are praised or berated because of what they did or did not do including the final verses of Matthew 25 picturing the Great Judgment. Many of the Pauline Epistles conclude with detailed instructions for right behavior, and the Epistle of James turns on the necessity for appropriate "doing."

Nevertheless, it is clear that doing, like knowing, is derivative. Right doing is possible only by faith, as Paul puts it in Galatians 2:11: "A man is not justified by works of the law but through faith in Jesus Christ, . . . because by works of the law shall no one be justified."[12] The statement of Jesus in John 12:47, "If anyone hears my sayings and does not keep them, I do not judge him; for I did not come to judge the world but to save the world,"[13] attests to the primacy of grace. The essence of the Incarnation turns on the fact that no one can keep the law, i.e., "do right," and thus what is needed is atonement, the restoration of broken relationships. The cross makes possible right doing, just as it makes possible right knowing.

As we turn, finally, to right "being," the matter is complicated in that the Bible does not use this term in a correlative fashion with "knowing" and "doing." Rather, it is necessary to search out the various forms and metaphors employed by biblical writers to express this concept. The most obvious is the use of "heart" to express essential "being." "Keep your heart with all vigilance; for from it flow the springs of life" (Prov. 4:35). It is upon the heart that God looks (I Sam. 16:7), and with the heart we believe (Rom. 10:10). The significance of the heart occurs over and over in the Psalms, and the promise of God in Ezekiel is, "I will give them one heart, and put a new spirit within them; I will take away the stony heart out of their flesh and give them a heart of flesh, that they may walk in my statutes and keep my ordinances and obey them" (11:19 ff.).

As can be seen, the Ezekiel passage establishes the

priority of the heart over both "knowing" and "doing," a priority that pervades the Scripture. It is in this vein that the Shema affirms, "Hear, O Israel: The Lord our God is one Lord; and you shall love the Lord your God with all your heart, and with all your soul, and with all your might" (Deut. 6:4-5). It is useful to note that the "words" are to be upon the heart, and the "teaching" of them to the children is experiential before it is conceptual.[14] In the New Testament, the beatitudes deal with being, including being "pure in heart" (Matt. 5:8), and it is out of the heart the evil arises (Matt. 15:19; Mark 7:21-23). Paul sees both obedience and faith arising from the heart (Rom. 6:17 and 10:10), and James appeals for purity of heart (4:8). Citations can be multiplied, but it is evident that quality of life is primary to quality of thought or quality of behavior. It is the person who has experienced newness of life who now sees things in the proper perspective, and whose actions attest to the restoration that has been wrought in the experience of forgiveness and reconciliation. So it is that pastoral care and counseling that focuses on being without disregarding knowing and doing is consistent with the biblical perspective, which sees all three as essential but also is clear on the basic priority of being over knowing and doing. The three attitudinal intentions of helping involve three basic words: "I instruct you," "I urge you," and "I love you." *Didascō, parakalō*, and *agapaō*, together with their cognate nouns, are woven through the whole fabric of biblical material. While all three are significant, there can be no doubt but that the primary word is *agapaō*.

## C

It is now possible to return to the import of text and narrative for the work of pastoral care and counseling, and discover the appropriate use of these passages in determining the practice of pastoral care. Those cited with primarily an instructional bent, e.g., "You shall know the truth" (John 8:31, 32), or the conversation with the woman at the well (John 4:1-42), set in the context of right being, help us understand the sense in which relationships are enhanced in the encounter with Jesus. Not often are the words just prior to the John 8 text cited in regard to knowing the "truth," but they are crucial. Jesus is speaking to those who believe in him, i.e., those whose faith has already emerged; he says, "If you continue in my word, you are truly my disciples, and you will know the truth, and the truth will make you free" (John 8:31, 32). Put in other words, the instruction is an essential means for structuring the faith rather than producing it. Faith, in the biblical sense, emerges in encounter and is nurtured in the instruction of the Word. In like manner, the conversation with the woman of Sychar enables us to see what happens to a person in this kind of encounter. The change of heart that was first evidenced by the woman and subsequently by her friends was based on their response to Jesus' grace, his care and concern for them which "set them free" to perceive the meaning in the event. Thus, far from providing a pattern for pastoral care and counseling in the sense of pressing for insight, these passages enable us to see the primary thrust of the pastoral ministry as reconciliation and change of heart.

In like manner, the texts and narratives cited as suggesting appropriate behavior as a means for resolving the tensions and difficulties of life, e.g., "Teach and urge these duties" (I Tim. 6:2), and the story of the rich young ruler (Luke 18:18 ff) illustrate the priority noted above. Paul, in the letter to Timothy, is setting forth the way in which the faith is structured in daily life. What he is saying presupposes a change of heart, the way in which Timothy and his people could discover more effective fashions for carrying out the implications of their response to grace.[15] It is the kind of instruction that is capable of appropriation precisely because the person has been empowered to "walk in newness of life" (Rom. 6:4). The same is true in the story of the rich young ruler. The intent of the narrative is to help us understand how impossible it is to inherit eternal life by our own efforts. So it is that Jesus does not tell him *the* thing that will accomplish this in the sense of when he does *this* he will have arrived. Rather, the import of the story is that only as he relinquishes any notion that he is capable of extricating himself from his predicament will there be any hope. The story, then, is told as representing the attitude of the disciples and us all. It is not what we *do* that enables us to inherit eternal life, although we would like to think so; rather it is what God has done that makes new life possible.[16]

Finally, the texts and narratives that move from the presupposition of reestablishing broken relationships are, as we have seen, more consistent with the biblical perspective of forgiveness and reconciliation than those which deal with right knowing and right doing. The concepts of bringing back together that which has been separated (Eph. 2:14,15) and justification by grace through faith (Rom. 3:23-25) are basic for the restoration of persons whose lives are distorted. By the same token, the story of the two brothers in Luke 15 describes the gracious forgiveness of God for both quite apart from their understanding the meaning of their behavior or doing those appropriate things which would merit approval. The forgiveness is primary in each instance, as evidenced by the father's going out of the house to meet first the

younger son and then the older. No penance is exacted
from the prodigal to make him "worthy" of the robe, the
ring, the shoes, or the banquet. No chiding is voiced to
the unforgiving elder son, only an affirmation of the
father's unchanging care of him as evidenced in
"everything I have is yours." The fact that the story ends
with no word of how long the younger stayed or whether
the older came in to the feast reminds us that God's grace
is not in any sense dependent on our response.

Nevertheless, to leave the matter here would be to
obscure the significance of "knowing" and "doing" as set
forth above. Thus, the texts and the narratives, however
consistent with the primary perspective of the Bible,
cannot be separated from the whole. It is to an exploration
of the fashion by which this more inclusive understanding
of biblical material informs process as well as principle in
pastoral care and counseling that this study is directed.
The following section sets forth the way in which this
larger perspective, which includes but also transcends
the specific texts and narratives, is employed as a basis for
the work of the minister.

## III

Thus far in our discussion we have looked at the biblical
priority in regard to the primary focus of pastoral care.
The primary principle upon which the discussion has
been based derives from the question, What is the Bible
as a whole intending to communicate, and how does this
intention manifest itself in this or that text or narrative in
such a way that each part participates in and emerges
from the unified whole? Only in dealing with this
question can the meaning of the various parts of Scripture

be rightly understood and incorporated into the life and work of the people of God.

### A

Seen in this light, it is clear that the Bible in all of its diversity of form and style deals essentially with God as creator, redeemer, and sustainer, and with wo/man as creature, sinner, and new creation as a consequence of response to grace by faith. In a word, the essence of biblical revelation is encompassed in its central theme regarding who God is and what He does, the nature of humankind and her/his tragic flaw, and the way God acts for and with humankind toward reconciliation and restoration, i.e., God, humankind, sin, and salvation.[17] Throughout, from beginning to end, the Bible deals with one facet or other of this quadratic emphasis, which draws from and informs the whole of Scripture. It is in this sense that all parts of the Bible are to be read not only in the context of the chapter or book in which they occur, but also in the context of the whole. It is this "interpretation of Scripture by Scripture"[18] which provides the minister with the only possible defense against subjectivity and the use of one or more texts or pericopes to support a position already determined. This does not mean, however, that every part fits neatly into the whole.[19] There are dimensions that resist such homogenization and remain forever at odds with other parts. It is here that the ultimate criterion derives from the faith of the interpreter. For many, including myself, this criterion is the meaning of the life, death, and resurrection of Jesus Christ.[20]

In the quadratic theme, God is revealed as holy and just in his infinite power. In this context, sin is always taken seriously; nor is there any notion of obscuring the misery and suffering that flow from it. At the same time,

God is seen as merciful and compassionate in his infinite love; in this context sin is overcome through sacrifice and death, and there is affirmation that the final word is the word of triumph and victory.

In like manner, humans are seen as creatures with creativity. Created in the image of God, they possess the capacity for choice, the awareness of consequences. As creatures with the divine *imago*, there is a fundamental need for relationships with self, others, and God. It is not possible to be human alone, as the Genesis text depicts so graphically (Gen. 2:18). At the same time, there is freedom, which makes possible the saying of yes or no in the complex issues of personal encounter and relationships.[21]

The "tragic flaw" of the human is his/her denial of this essential nature by striving to live other than as a creature with creativity; in the attempt to be more than s/he in fact is, s/he breaks the essential relationships with God, others, and self, and moves toward loneliness, isolation, and death in the painful and destructive bondage of evil both self-made and imposed. This bondage produces a longing for release, for a deliverance from the guilt, failure, and death caused by sin; at the same time there is an inhibiting fear and resistance to being discovered which perpetuates the isolation and prevents the very relationship that can bring restoration.

It is in response to this wretched state of affairs that God is revealed as taking the initiative toward the restoration of broken relationships in his actions of judgment and grace. In this sense, judgment represents his holiness and grace represents his love. Together, judgment and grace constitute forgiveness and the offer of life. The person may say no, in which case the bondage remains. Nevertheless, the person may say yes, and in

this yes experience the reestablishing of broken relationships, becoming a "new creature" able to forgive and be
forgiven, to love and be loved.[22]

Finally, in this basic theme of God, humankind, sin,
and salvation, the sequence is logical but not inherent. To
be sure, God has priority in all things; but any
contemplation of God apart from the created order
remains speculative at best, however fascinating it may
be. The opening words of Genesis, "In the beginning God
created the heavens and the earth" (Gen. 1:1), forever
focus our attention on the interrelatedness of the
quadratic theme. From a biblical point of view it is
impossible to talk about any one aspect of this theme
without involving the other three. The separation into
parts is solely for the purpose of discussion toward clearer
understanding, but such separation remains essentially
artificial and inevitably moves into the whole even as it
draws from the whole.

## B

In the matter of implications of this basic theme to the
principle and practice of pastoral care, it is possible to
examine the various texts and pericopes in the context of
this unified theme alone, and so determine their meaning
for the work of ministry. However, the task is facilitated
by attention to the sub-themes that are woven into this
basic strand and that recur over and again in first one
setting and then another. As is true in the basic quadratic
theme of the Bible, all the subordinate themes are
interdependent, all relate to and draw from all the rest.
The value of the theme is seen in the perspective that it
provides for the whole; by the same token, each theme is
but a part or aspect of the whole, and never exists in and of
itself.

The notion of "themes" is not a novel one, nor is it free from danger. Like "salvation history" and the "unity of the Bible," this concept gained tremendous impetus in the forties and fifties, although it did not originate with that period. In 1938 Gerhard von Rad pointed to various themes in *The Problem of the Hexateuch*. Martin Noth in *A History of Pentateuchal Traditions* identifies five "major themes" in the material. John Bright makes a case for three distinctive "features" or themes in biblical material, i.e., "election," "covenant," and "promise." Walter Eichrodt finds a unifying theme in the concept of "covenant."[23] Other references are ready to hand, but these suffice to indicate the value of biblical themes as a means for gaining a better or more adequate understanding of Scripture. The use of this concept as a factor in determining the implications of biblical material for the work of the minister is influenced by but not confined to the various emphases noted in such writings, which are not always in basic agreement. In the matter of unity, for example, my own position is much more in accord with von Rad than with Martin Noth, who sees the themes in the pentateuchal tradition as unrelated in a historical sense even though they came to be related as the texts of Scripture were woven together.[24]

There are, as we noted, dangers in the identification and utilization of biblical themes in the interpretation of Scripture and, particularly, in drawing implications for the work of ministry. Essentially the risk is subjectivity, the temptation to decide upon a "likely theme" and then search biblical material for texts to support it. That I am categorically opposed to such a procedure has already been made clear in my rejection of finding various texts and narratives to support a particular approach in pastoral procedure without subjecting them to scrutiny in the context of the essential purpose of the Bible. But being opposed to this pitfall and avoiding it are certainly not the same thing. Although I have attempted to guard against this kind of subjectivity, my own work with biblical themes is an ongoing one, and it is possible that the publication of this study will be the occasion for constructive criticism that will enrich the understanding of us all.

Alongside such subjectivity there is the danger that in identifying certain themes, others will be omitted that would prove helpful in informing procedure in pastoral care and counseling. In that sense, I make no brief for the list presented as being exhaustive. The fact is that I have worked, and am working, with various other themes and find them stimulating and useful. The limitation here is utilitarian, dictated by the necessity to keep the book within reasonable bounds. The limitation is justified by reason of the fact that these themes are representative and illustrative of the central theme of the Bible but in no sense replace it. The unifying factor is the central theme, not any of the subordinate themes. Thus, while the addition of one or more themes might prove beneficial, such an addition would in no sense alter or change the whole.

All the themes utilized here are rooted in the Yahwist material, beginning with the primeval history and moving through the patriarchal history. Thence the themes are traced to and through the New Testament, noting their manifestation in various forms and circumstances. This tracing, of course, is suggestive rather than exhaustive since to do the latter would defeat the purpose of the book which is to move from the theme to implications for the work of ministry.

The use of the Yahwist material is deliberate as in it the basic thrust of the Bible is set forth in brief but comprehensive fashion.[25] Moreover, in the primeval history, which is a unique contribution of the Yahwist, there is a simple yet profound account of the basic quadratic theme of the Bible. Here we see God's creativity and care, wo/man's potential and brokenness, and God's promise of reconciliation. As von Rad put it:

The meagerness of his resources is truly amazing, and yet this narrator's point of view encompasses the whole of human life with all its heights and depths. With unrivaled objectivity he has made man the subject of his presentation—both the riddles and conflicts of his visible acts and ways of behaving as well as the mistakes and muddles in the secret of his heart. He among the biblical writers is the great psychologist. However, he is concerned, not with man who with his desires and despair believes himself to be alone in the world, but rather with man to whom the living God has been revealed and who therefore has become the object of divine address, a divine act, and therefore a divine judgment and divine salvation. Thus, in the primeval history he subjects the great problems of humanity to the light of revelation: creation and nature, sin and suffering, man and wife, fraternal quarrels, international confusion, etc. But above all, he investigates God's activities in the beginnings of Israel, both their visible wonders and their hidden mysteries.[26]

It is certain that the Yahwist material is ordered to speak to the nation in the tenth century, B.C., and the various themes such as God's love, sin and punishment, selection of the younger brother, the identifying God as the provider of food and clothing, and so on were designed to interpret theologically the meaning of the heritage and the import of God's actions for contemporary issues and decisions. Yet, it is precisely this ability to think theologically about life in all its intricacies, and especially in regard to the way persons discover their identity and purpose in the light of God, that makes the Yahwist material relevant not only for his time but for all time. To be sure, we stand on this side of the Cross, and can see many things far more clearly than was possible for this ancient theologian; nevertheless, his insight into the basic issues of life is incredibly sound, and adumbrates the unfolding and promise that we know in the structure of biblical material.[27] Although our tracing of the themes will not be confined to the Yahwist material, it is nonetheless rooted there, as has been noted. No attempt is made here to identify or distinguish between other strands in the Old Testament, and the same is true in references to the Gospels and New Testament material. To undertake such an exercise would divert us from our primary task. The basic principle employed is the use of the material in terms of its inherent meaning, avoiding distortion by the imposition of alien ideas.

In this context, the themes that are explored in the chapters that follow are: (1) initiative and freedom, (2) fear and faith, (3) conformity and rebellion, (4) death and rebirth, and (5) risk and redemption. As each is introduced, a more detailed discussion of its meaning is presented and illustrated in pastoral conversations.

## IV

Our final task before turning to the several themes is to explore briefly the nature of pastoral care and counseling and to describe the pastoral conversations that are set forth in each chapter as a means of demonstrating the implications of a particular theme for the actual work of the minister.

In the biblical sense, pastoral care is that function of the people of God wherein we "bear one another's burdens, and so fulfil the law of Christ" (Gal. 6:2) as the means for participating in the process of reconciliation. Pastoral counseling is rightly understood only in the context of pastoral care. So it is that we look first at the general nature of pastoral care and then at the more specific nature of pastoral counseling.

The "bearing of burdens" is not something done simply "for" others; rather it is a corporate venture done "with" others, since "each man will have to bear his own load"(Gal. 6:5). Every member of the *laos* of God participates to some degree or other in pastoral ministry, just as each is the recipient of pastoral care. It is a process whereby we listen with gentleness and patience, speak with truth and love, hold out a hand in time of loneliness and fear, sit in silence through the long night watches, and rejoice when the shadow of distress is dissolved in the warm sun of deliverance. Pastoral care takes place in all sorts and fashions of circumstance. It is present in a phone call, in a conversation over the backyard fence, in a busy marketplace, or the quiet whiteness of a hospital room. It is evident in a card received in the mail, in a covered dish prepared at the time of bereavement, in an errand run or a child kept for the afternoon. Such ministries are not usually identified by the person performing them or the person receiving them as "pastoral care." Rather, they are seen as simple acts of mercy, a cup of cold water, part and parcel of being sensitive to need and meeting the need in the way most available. So it is that if most people are asked for instances wherein they have participated in pastoral care, they will shake their heads and find no ready answer. Perhaps it is just as well, although there is genuine value in persons' becoming more conscious of the meaning of what it is they do, and more intentional in discovering new ways to bear one another's burdens. One of the encouraging dimensions of our day is the participation of lay persons in seminars and workshops in ministry toward more effective ways of being of help in varieties of situations. It is in this sense that the priesthood of all believers takes renewed form and substance as the essence of pastoral care.

As we have seen, such pastoral care is not concerned primarily with producing right knowing or right doing, although neither of these is ignored. Rather, there is throughout the basic intention of reestablishing broken relationships, of healing the wounds of loneliness and grief, of loving and forgiving in the context of truth and grace. There will always, of course, be things for the person to understand just as there will always be things to be done. But these are seen as derivative in the primary focus on encounter, on relationships, on reconciliation. The person is always more important than the problem, and the relationship is more important than the solution. Many of the problems of life are insoluble on their own terms: lost opportunities do not come again; death may be postponed but not avoided; decisions that offer pain, however made, cannot be escaped. In the biblical sense triumph comes not in the altering of the externals, although at times this is needed; rather the true success comes in the transformation of the person in a relationship of love and forgiveness so that s/he is able to deal creatively with any situation (cf. Phil. 4:13). So it is that presence is more important than programmed solution as the person discovers the basic meaning of "I will fear no evil for thou art with me" (Ps. 23:4). The seemingly whimsical but actually profound request from *Alice in Wonderland,* "Don't just do something, stand there," is a fundamental word of truth for this kind of bearing of burdens.

Broadly based, then, pastoral care is the ongoing process of ministry in which all persons engage to some extent or other. The minister, as a part of the *laos* of God, participates in this burden bearing in varieties of forms. As a minister, however, s/he is designated both as one who enables persons to engage in pastoral care, and as one who is responsible for disciplined study toward developing a competence that is not necessarily expected of the members of the congregation. Much of the minister's work will be of the order of pastoral care, short-term burden-bearing and nurture in situational occasions of need. At the same time, the minister engages in pastoral counseling that is based upon but not identical with pastoral care. The difference is one of degree, not of kind. Pastoral counseling is that function of ministry wherein the minister and the parishioner or parishioners focus in a concentrated and atypical fashion on the situation of the latter toward providing the kind of support structure and relational encounter that will enable the person once again to draw nourishment from the on-going processes of life. In this sense, pastoral counseling is expendable, its only goal being to arrive at the point where such an atypical relationship is no longer needed.[28]

Pastoral counseling is needed when, under certain circumstances, the person(s) are so wounded, so cut off from the life-giving relationships, so deeply entrenched behind the deadly facades of destructive behavior that concentrated attention is required for restoration. A figure that has become familiar in our time which helps to clarify this point is the life support systems of the astronauts. Ordinarily, these persons live in an environment that provides for the sustaining of life; but in the alien environment of space, atypical and temporary measures are needed if they are to live. The same life-giving substances are required, but the form for providing them is extraordinary. Everything is concentrated, and the process itself is artificial. The ultimate purpose is to sustain the person until s/he is restored to the ordinary and on-going sources of life. At such a time, the cumbersome and ungainly support systems are no longer needed and can be laid aside, since the purpose of these devices is not to exist for themselves, but to enable the persons to return to the natural processes of life. So, also, pastoral counseling has as its primary purpose to support the person(s) when needed but no longer.[29]

In the case material included in the following chapters, some of the situations can properly be understood as pastoral care and others as pastoral counseling. Several set forth the first meeting concerned with some problem or issue between the minister and the parishioner(s), while others represent longer-term counseling on a regular basis. Some involve both husband and wife in marriage counseling, others portray pastoral care of families, and still others represent conversations between the minister and one parishioner.

In recent years we have become increasingly aware of the inter-involvement of all persons with other significant members of their families, and that factor is evident in all the case material. This is true whether or not every member of the family is actually present in the interview. This position differs from that of some family therapists who insist upon seeing all of the family. While my own understanding of the care of persons has been enriched by the contemporary emphasis on family involvement, this has not negated the value of my experiences of participating in the growth and nurture of persons on a one-to-one basis apart from their families of origin. Since many of the students in seminary are separated from their families by hundreds if not thousands of miles, there is no opportunity for siblings and parents to be literally present. Even so, I am constantly aware of the fact that those persons are "in the room" and these basic relationships inform all that happens in the pastoral conversation. Through the encounter between the minister and the person, new patterns of relating can emerge so that the person is set free from the damaging structures that played a greater or lesser part in the current distress.[30]

Most ministers will not engage in family therapy in the technical sense of that term as this process is highly intricate and requires more time and skill than the parish minister has opportunity to acquire. Nevertheless, every minister is constantly involved in family structures and the quality of his/her pastoral care is enhanced precisely as s/he takes seriously the family systems theories and therapeutic principles that have been articulated and demonstrated in clinical practice in recent years.[31] It is in this sense that every pastoral conversation is informed by an awareness of the interlocking involvement of the person(s) with significant others, an awareness that sets aside any notion that somehow or other the "problem" exists solely "inside the parishioner's skin," so to speak. Rather, as we have seen in discussing the biblical material, all human difficulties are relational and can be resolved only in a restoration of broken relationships.

# Chapter Two
## *Initiative and Freedom*

We have seen that the basic theme of the Bible is concerned with God, humankind, sin, and salvation and that all parts of Scripture derive from and contribute to this central motif. As we turn to a consideration of various sub-themes, we do so in order to gain a clearer understanding of this basic theme for the work of ministry in pastoral care and counseling. Always, however, we remain conscious of the whole of which these themes are only parts. The first sub-theme is initiative and freedom.

### I

"It is not good that the man should be alone" (Gen 2:18) is the key text that calls attention to the corporate existence of persons. There follows the account of the creation of the animals; and after the man had given names to all of them which was possible as he discovered their essence, his loneliness was greater still, "for the man there was not found a helper fit for him" (Gen. 2:20). It is then that the creation of the woman shatters the loneliness and isolation. "This at last is bone of my bones and flesh of my flesh; she shall be called Woman (*ishshah*), because she was taken out of Man (ish)" (Gen. 2:23). [1]

In Genesis 3 the account of the temptation and fall results in isolation and alienation. The man and the woman who had the capacity to live as creatures with creativity misuse their freedom in attempting to be more than they in fact were; and the result is fear, which drives them to hide, to build barriers that separate them from themselves, from each other, and from God.

It is in this context that the theme of initiative and freedom emerges as the polar dimensions for the reestablishing of the broken relationships. "And they heard the sound of the Lord God walking in the garden in the cool of the day, and the man and his wife hid themselves from the presence of the Lord God among the trees of the garden. But the Lord God called to the man, and said to him, 'Where are you?' " (Gen. 3:8, 9). The question is the primary factor in the bringing back into being that which was lost in the fall. Indeed, the entire remainder of the biblical narrative is an extension of and commentary on the call of God, "Adam, where are you?" which reaches its culmination in Jesus' statement, "For the Son of man came to seek and to save the lost" (Luke 19:10).

God's initiative in relating to Adam begins in the promises of the Garden and is seen most clearly in the concept of covenant. Indeed, in the biblical sense, covenant can be understood only in terms of the relationship between God and wo/man as continually God moves toward the effecting of the community between person with person, and persons with God. The overt statement of covenant follows the flood when God speaks to Noah, "Behold I establish my covenant with you and your descendants." It is repeated in Genesis 12:2 as God summons Abram from Haran and promises that he will become a great nation.[2]

46

The coming of the Old Testament prophets continues the search for Adam. Over and over the Word of God comes to his people in the midst of their distress and dismay to bring the promise of deliverance and restoration, to enable them to turn from darkness to light, from death to life. The culminating passage in the Old Testament is Jeremiah 31:31-34:

Behold, the days are coming, says the Lord, when I will make a new covenant with the house of Israel and the house of Judah, not like the covenant which I made with their fathers when I took them by the hand to bring them out of the land of Egypt, my covenant which they broke, though I was their husband, says the Lord. But this is the covenant which I will make with the house of Israel after those days, says the Lord: I will put my law within them, and I will write it upon their hearts; and I will be their God, and they shall be my people. And no longer shall each man teach his neighbor and each his brother, saying "Know the Lord," for they shall all know me, from the least of them to the greatest, says the Lord; for I will forgive their iniquity, and I will remember their sin no more.

Throughout the entire scope of covenant, the basic factor is God's initiative; it is he who moves toward wo/man to reestablish the broken relationships, it is he who again and again renews the covenant which wo/man ignores or breaks. The meaning of covenant is fulfilled in the Incarnation, the coming of him who is "Emmanuel," God with us (Matt. 1:23), who, on the night in which he was betrayed, took bread, blessed and broke it, and gave it to his disciples; and the same way the cup, saying, "This cup is the new covenant in my blood" (I Cor. 11:25; cf. also Matt. 26:26-29; Mark 14:22-25; Luke 22:17-19).[3]

The biblical concept of God's initiative, however, is always set against the corresponding concept of human freedom. "The Yahwist does not picture the man and the woman dancing as puppets on the end of a string tied to the great puppeteer in the sky. Rather, God respects human freedom; and by respecting human freedom, he runs the risk implied in a genuine call to obedience."[4] The roots of this freedom, bound up in being created in the "image of God" (Gen. 1:26-27), are clearly seen in the Yahwist's description of the conversation between God and the man in Genesis 2:16-17. "And the Lord God commanded the man, saying, 'You may freely eat of every tree of the garden; but of the tree of the knowledge of good and evil you shall not eat, for in the day that you eat of it you shall die.' " Here the possibility of choice is unmistakable; Adam may decide either way. With the negative decision that followed, however, the freedom is forfeited. The bondage that ensues is broken only by the word of reconciliation that comes as God searches for Adam, who is hiding among the trees of the garden. Paradoxically, the new freedom that comes with the offer of relationships may be used to turn back into non-freedom. Rather than responding in openness, wo/man may resist the offer of reconciliation and retreat once again behind the facades of hypocrisy.[5]

The three references to clothing in Genesis 2 and 3 present a graphic account of the meaning of freedom. In Genesis 2:25 we read: "And the man and his wife were both naked, and were not ashamed." Here, there are no barriers, no facades, no "dividing walls of hostility" (Eph. 2:14). After eating the forbidden fruit, however, "they sewed fig leaves together and made themselves aprons" (Gen. 3:7). This is the beginning of the hiding, of the deceit and the "mechanisms of defense" which continue throughout human history.[6] The surprising turn of events that gives continued meaning to the concept of freedom comes following the encounter of the Lord God with the man and his wife. It might be supposed that God's interest would be directed toward the taking away of the barriers so that the open relationships could be experienced again. Certainly, in an ultimate sense, this is just what is envisioned. Nevertheless, this is not to be accomplished apart from their freedom to say no rather than yes. For rather than stripping off the aprons made of fig leaves or allowing them to wilt and drop away of their own accord, the Lord God "made for Adam and for his wife garments of skins, and clothed them" (Gen. 3:21). Unexpectedly, the Lord God participates in their hiding in the kind of gesture that assures their right to remain hidden until they respond to the word of invitation freely. The freedom to reject relationships persists throughout the entire Old Testament. A poignant reference to the capacity to say no is found in Hosea 11:2: "The more I called them, the more they went from me; they kept sacrificing to the Baals, and burning incense to idols."

In the New Testament the theme occurs again and again. "He came to his own home, and his own people received him not" (John 1:11). In John 6:66, 67 there is the account that "after this many of his disciples drew back and no longer went about with him. Jesus said to the twelve, 'Will you also go away?' " It was a choice they were free to make, and it is certain that had they decided to do so, he would not have stopped them, just as he did not stop the rich young ruler (Matt. 19:16-22, and others) or Judas on the night in which he was betrayed (John 13:27-30). Correspondingly, Jesus continually was asked or forced to leave and always did so. Luke 8:37 is a characteristic verse: "Then all the people of the surrounding country of the Gerasenes asked him to depart from them; . . . so he got into the boat and returned." (See also Luke 4:30; 9:56; and others.)

The scope of initiative and freedom is summarized in Revelation 3:20, "Behold, I stand at the door and knock; if anyone hears my voice and opens the door, I will come in to him and eat with him, and he with me." This image, which has been depicted by Hunt in the painting "Christ at the Door," speaks graphically of the initiative in the knocking at the door—and of the freedom that the door be opened only from within. It is as the door is opened that the relationship is reestablished in the symbol of eating, which represents the communion in which there are no barriers or facades to separate persons from themselves, from others, or from God.

## II

We turn now to a discussion of certain implications of initiative and freedom for the work of the minister. As is true of all the themes, this one impinges on pastoral care and counseling at every point, and in later chapters these relationships are identified in a different context. Here, however, our attention is directed to the meaning of "contract" in pastoral care and counseling where the minister takes the initiative in the pastoral relationship.[7] Most simply put, "contract" designates willingness, however strong or weak, however overtly stated or covertly manifested, of two (or more) persons at any given time and within whatever limitations may be set to concentrate on the distresses or difficulties that beset one (or more) of them. From the point of view of the parishioner(s), the contract represents an openness to the pastor, a decision made at whatever level to reveal aspects of the self and to wrestle with the ambiguities, failures, and hurts of life. In practically every instance the contract is conditional and represents all manner of ambiguity and ambivalence. There is at one and the same time a desire for help and a resistance to being helped. The nature of this distress may be stated as outside the persons, i.e., "if they or it were different, there would be no problem," or within the person(s), i.e., "I am distressed in this or that way." But however the situation may be presented, the contract represents the person(s) saying overtly or covertly, "I have this problem, and I want you to help me." Just as the statement of admission of the problem is generally ambiguous, so is the notion of the meaning of help ambiguous. Ordinarily, there is a longing for some change in circumstance, some relieving of pressure, some deliverance from consequences of previous acts, some miraculous intervention that will wipe the slate clean. The essence throughout is the acknowledgment of distress and the desire for relief in which the assistance of another person is sought.

From the point of view of the pastor, the contract depends on a willingness, however determined, to accept the request for help. There exists the same ambiguity and ambivalence that mark the attitude of the parishioner. On the one hand, there may be a genuine desire to be of help, while on the other there may be reservations of all sorts. These reservations may arise from not being sure just what to do, from personal inability to participate in the bearing of the burdens of others, or from a radical difference in definition of what constitutes "help" as compared with that held by the parishioner.[8] The contract is effected when the pastor, despite any reservations that may be present, agrees to participate with the person in dealing with the disturbing situation as best s/he can. The contract is always subject to limitations such as how long the concentration on the problem will be, how often it will be undertaken, what kinds of expectations are legitimate, and so on. Not all of these are necessarily dealt with overtly at the outset, but until some mutuality and clarity is reached, the process tends to move at cross purposes. Moreover, the contract needs to be "renegotiated" from time to time; and in any event it may be terminated by either person at any time whether or not the other person wishes.

It would be incorrect to suppose that the contract is often or ordinarily spelled out in some detail, although aspects of it may be.[9] In most instances, there is the barest agreement between pastor and parishioner: "I need your help," and "I am willing to help if I can." Nevertheless, the understanding of the implications of the contractual arrangement is crucial for the minister who engages in the cure of souls lest s/he inadvertently offer more than s/he can produce and thus raise false hopes and expectations on the part of the parishioner.

Thus far in the discussion, we have been dealing primarily with those circumstances where the parishioner comes to the pastor for help, however defined. In such instances, there can be no question about the person's willingness or desire to enter a specific relationship even though the request and the reception may be very tentative or ambiguous. Here, the only task for the minister is to determine whether s/he feels able to help, and if so, in what fashion and to what extent.

The matter is much more complex, however, when the minister takes the initiative to go unbidden to the person. Then it is that a knowledge of the way the contract is established is absolutely essential if the pastoral call is to be effective in any sense at all. It is to this question that we devote the remainder of the discussion in the following section, leaving for chapter 5 a more detailed consideration of contract when the person comes to the minister with the problem.

Pastoral calls initiated by the minister concern persons in three general categories: (1) those persons in whom known difficulty exists (although it may); (2) those persons whose difficulty is openly manifest such as the sick, the bereaved; and (3) those persons whose difficulty is known or suspected, but who have not made any overt mention of it, let alone requested help in the matter, such as those experiencing alcoholism, unwanted pregnancy, severed personal relationships in a family, i.e. parent-child, husband-wife. In the discussion and case material following we look first at a call on a family where no known problem exists and then a call in a hospital where the parishioner is awaiting surgery. In each instance the focus is upon the implications of initiative and freedom for understanding the contract between the minister and the parishioners.

It is commonplace today to note that the idea of what is usually termed routine pastoral calling is largely ignored by most ministers. The reasons for this shift in emphasis from the ordinary practice of a generation ago is generally put in some such terms as, "People are too scattered, and too much time is wasted in trying to find them," or "People know where I am and that I am available, and will call on me when they need me," or "I am willing to go when there is some obvious distress such as sickness, hospitalization, bereavement, but beyond that there are more significant things to do than ringing doorbells where no one is at home, or, if they are, they do not want to see the minister." However much validity there may be in any or all such sentiments, it is likely that a deeper cause lies at the root of the matter, namely, that ministers are no longer sure of what it is that they are to do on a "routine" call, and resist any notion of "wasting time" by idle conversation about the weather or the trivialities of everyday life.

When the concept of initiative is taken seriously, however, no such neglect of pastoral visitation is possible. It is instructive, if a bit ironic, that the value of a call in the home has been brought to our attention anew by contemporary family therapists. The opportunity to be with people where they live, to understand their "life space," to experience the lines of force in the family system and their effect upon each member of the family is crucial for effective pastoral care. While most ministers will not engage in family therapy, as we have already noted, it is certain that an awareness of family relationships is essential to effective pastoral care. Moreover, the minister has a distinct advantage over colleagues in the other helping professions. S/he may ring doorbells, enter hospital rooms, visit in offices, call by telephone, and in varieties of ways take the initiative to stand with persons in all sorts of circumstances. This does not mean that the initiative will always be welcome or that the minister will always be able to be of help if the need arises. At times the parishioners may refuse to "open the door" of their lives, even while they open the door to their homes. Or it may be that the minister will be inept in dealing with the opportunities that present themselves. Nevertheless, taking seriously the privilege of initiative means that the minister has the opportunity to go while the distress may not yet be in a critical stage, and this is considerable advantage over colleagues who often are called only after the issues have become so painful that there is little other choice.

In addition, the pastor-initiated call is a tangible demonstration of the "good news" that resources are available. Like bringing bread to one who is starving or light to one groping in darkness, it is the act of offering that which can make life meaningful. In the biblical sense, it is the searching for Adam, the leaving the ninety-and-nine to look for the lost sheep, the knocking at the door, the Incarnation. It is not predicated on the assurance of positive response; it may, in fact, provoke resentment and hostility, as we shall see more fully in chapter 6. Nevertheless, this initiative is the basic factor in pastoral care undertaken in the spirit of him who "came to seek and to save that which was lost" (Luke 19:10).

The danger in all this is that in the coming, the integrity of the person(s) visited is violated. Put in terms of the biblical theme, the freedom of the person(s) to say no can never be set aside or ignored. The coming is redemptive only insofar as it represents a total willingness to be rebuffed and to turn away, however sadly, only to try again if opportunity permits or if there is some indication on the part of the person that the door is opening. The tragic fact for most ministers in the context of Revelation 3:20 ("Behold I stand at the door and knock; if anyone hears my voice and opens the door, I will come in") is that on the one hand they give up knocking altogether, which is too often the case, or misread the verse: "Behold I stand at the door with a fireaxe; if anyone will not open the door, I will chop it down and come in, anyhow!" The first ignores the meaning of initiative, and the second ignores the meaning of freedom. It is as the two are brought together in the imagery of knocking and waiting for the door to be opened that a true ministry is realized.[10]

In any call where the minister takes the initiative, and where no known difficulty exists, the critical factor for pastoral effectiveness is the willingness to follow the leads of the person(s). This means that the minister will most certainly not probe in the lives of the parishioners in the hope of finding some issue with which to deal; by the same token, it means that the minister is prepared to shift from an informal conversation to one that engages the parishioner on a more personal level if s/he indicates some hurt or concern is troubling. The minister properly assumes that the person is characterized by any of the following situations: (1) the person may, in fact, have no difficulty that needs discussing; (2) the person may have such a difficulty but not want to discuss it; (3) the person may have such a difficulty and want to discuss it but not right now; (4) the person may have such a difficulty and want to discuss it right now but not with the minister; and finally, (5) the person may have such a difficulty, and want to discuss it right now with the minister. The circumstance producing the fifth factor, which is the only one requesting a contract, may not emerge until the conversation is underway; that is, the parishioner may decide to bring the matter up without having previously intended to do so. It is the pastor's ability to shift his/her focus to the area designated by the person that is a mark of effective pastoral care. This is true no matter what the agenda brought by the minister, i.e., simply to call, or to ask the person to undertake some task, or to invite the person to attend worship services, or to welcome him/her to the community, and so on.

The essential dimension of the beginning of an initiated pastoral call is the minister's clear definition of why s/he is there. The notion that one should engage in idle small talk before "getting around to why I am here" is misleading and dishonest, leaving the person(s) wondering "what on earth do you suppose s/he's up to?" If the purpose of the call is to ask that the person(s) consider some task or responsibility in the church or community, then that needs to be said at the outset, else the minister will not truly hear anything that is being said by the parishioner(s) as s/he waits for an opening to lay out such an agenda item. If, on the other hand, the purpose of the call is simply to visit, inasmuch as the minister hopes to maintain as close a touch as possible, then that needs to be said. Neither of these purposes precludes the parishioner's introducing agenda items as appropriate; both give an essential aspect of genuine encounter which makes constructive relationships possible.

The establishing of the contract can be identified in the awareness that all pastoral conversation, whether counseling or visiting, is comprised of a series of definitions. The minister states who s/he is and the purpose of the visit; the parishioner in turn defines him/her self, and the encounter is engaged.[11] It is as the minister is sensitive to the parishioner(s)' self definitions that the conversation is truly pastoral. As long as the definitions indicate that the person is coping appropriately with the issues of life, the only proper attitude on the part of the minister is rejoicing. But when the parishioner states or implies that something is, to whatever extent, amiss the minister hears this as a clue toward the possibility of a different level of conversation.

The parishioner(s) may request a contract in one of two ways, overt and covert. The overt request is the simple statement to the effect, "I am worried about this and would like to discuss it with you." This "opening the door" may come at any point, and on the basis of the minister's situation at the time s/he may say yes or no to the request.[12] The covert request is far more subtle, and often overlooked by the minister. This request occurs when the statements of the parishioner no longer deal with the facts or situations being discussed, but with the effect of these facts or situations upon him or her. Put in other words, when the parishioner moves from the "what" to the "how," there is a covert although real request for a contract. Such a shift happens in various ways. For example, a parishioner may have been speaking about a son in college, where he is, what courses he is taking, and the like, and then as the conversation progresses say, "I sort of wonder if he's really doing what he wants to do." Now the focus is not on what is happening, but how this situation is affecting the parent. This type of opening the door may also come at any point in the conversation; and in like manner as above the minister may say yes or no to the request.

The contract is terminated by either person. It may be terminated by the minister overtly by his/her having to leave for whatever reason, or by his/her suggesting that they continue the discussion at a later time in a more controlled environment such as his office where the possibility of interruption is reduced. Unfortunately, the contract is often terminated covertly by the minister because of his/her inability to listen to the person any longer. Such a termination usually happens without the minister's realizing it at the time but recognizing it in retrospect as s/he thinks back over what happened. The ordinary marks of such minister-imposed termination are seen in the giving of advice, proffering some facile reassurance, asking questions that turn away from the parishioner, or engaging in a theoretical discussion of the matter raised by the parishioner.

On the other hand, the contract may be terminated by the parishioner's overt indication that s/he does not wish to pursue the matter further or would like to interrupt the conversation at any point and take it up later. More often the contract is concluded covertly, as evidenced by the parishioner's moving from the "how" to the "what," usually by making a statement regarding the solution of the problem, shifting the subject, or asking questions about the pastor. In light of the concept of freedom as we have been understanding it, it is essential that the minister be sensitive not only to the covert requesting of the contract, but also to its termination.

## III

In the two verbatim reconstructions that follow, the general principles inherent in the initiative-and-freedom theme, illustrated by the minister's calling on parishioners while recognizing the necessity for taking care to preserve their freedom of response, are discussed.

### A

The first involves a call on a family, a John and Adele X and their two teen-age girls, Sarah and Martha. The minister who presented this verbatim for discussion and evaluation indicated that he had gone to their home on a Tuesday evening about 7:45. His only purpose in going, as he put it, "was simply to visit with them inasmuch as I do not get to keep in touch with my parishioners adequately if the only time I speak to them is on Sunday." He noted that he had put an announcement in the bulletin that he would be visiting "in that neighborhood" throughout the coming week, but that he had not made a specific appointment with the X's prior to calling. (In the verbatim reconstruction J = John, A = Adele, M = Martha, P = Pastor. The dots—" . . ."—indicate pauses, not omissions of words.)

I went by to call on the X's as a part of my general routine calling, by which I try to visit every family in their home at least once a year. It was about 7:45 P.M. when I rang the doorbell. After a few minutes the door was opened by Mrs. X.

1.P.     Good evening, Mrs. X. It's Frank Johnson, and I'd like to come in and visit with you and the family if it is convenient.

2.A.     Uh, why yes, . . . yes . . . do come right in. Sarah's gone, but John and Martha are here. John, it's the minister, and he's here to visit with us.

3.J.     *(Standing up from chair and walking toward the entrance hall.)* Hello, Reverend. Come on in and have a seat. Let me turn off this TV; boy, there's not much on these days . . .

4.P.     *(As we were seated.)* That's sure the truth. . . . How are all of you getting along?

5.A.     Fine . . . just fine. You'll have to pardon the looks of this living room; I've not had time to pick up much today, and these three really give it a "lived in" look!

6.P.     Don't give it a thought; as a matter of fact, I feel right at home! Guess it's pretty much of an endless task to keep it straight.

7.A.     That's about the story . . .

In the opening part of the conversation, several aspects stand out which relate to "initiative and freedom" and the matter of the contract. As already noted, some sort of definition is needed at the beginning of any interview initiated by the minister simply so that the persons have an opportunity to know what is going on. In this verbatim, the minister gives only the barest hint regarding why he is there. In every pastoral counseling interview, the introductory remarks may be the most crucial for the course of what happens later. The same is generally true in a pastoral call, although by reason of cultural "games" it is probably easier to overcome idle chitchat on the way to more substantive discourse. "How have things been going?" is better than "How are all of you getting along?" since this leaves them with the option of talking about themselves, the weather, the church, politics, or whatever. At the same time, apart from some notion of what the minister is doing there, they are by necessity guarded. Does he have a hidden agenda? If so, what is it? Such thoughts are inevitably distracting; and thus, somewhat self-consciously, Mrs. X makes a comment about the state of disarray in the living room.

This apology raises the whole point of whether any pastoral call should be made unannounced. Many ministers who still make general calls believe that it is better to "catch people where they are," and thus have a more realistic visit. Seen in the light of "initiative and freedom," however, this tends to violate the person's right to refuse the call if it is not desired, or to "pick up" the house as well as his/her own perspective in anticipation of the visit. Phoning ahead accomplishes not only a means for giving the person the right to say no, but also prevents the waste of time ringing a doorbell where no one is at home. The phone call, itself, provides opportunity for definition. "I am in the neighborhood and would like to stop by to see you for a few minutes if that is convenient. Nothing particular on my mind; just realized that I'd not had the opportunity to talk with you for some time and would like to do so." Such a call made not too far in advance does not subtly require that elaborate preparations be made for the visit such as refreshments, spic-and-span housecleaning, and the like. At the same time, the persons have ample opportunity to demur, or to shift toward receiving the caller. What will be involved in this shift will vary from person to person; the primary factor is that the parishioner's freedom is maintained.

The minister's response in 6 P is adequate, although the initial admonition is questionable. However well intended, all injunctions that "prescribe" feelings, such as "Now, don't worry" or "Don't let that bother you" and the like, communicate to the parishioner that it is inappropriate to voice what is actually happening to him/her. It is certain that the feelings do not leave; rather they must be repressed while the person searches for more acceptable attitudes. Our cultural patterns have strongly influenced us here as we attempt to resolve the struggles of others by superficial reassurance: "Now, now. Everything will turn out all right, you'll see," or admonitions for positive thinking: "Just look on the bright side, and put those worries out of your mind." At base, this is saying, "I don't really want to hear where you are; say something pleasant, for that makes me feel better, and if you have to cry, please do so after I've gone." If confronted with such a concept, most of us would reject or deny it, vowing that what we intended to do was help. The minister who is sensitive to the person's inner feelings, however, will not fall into such a trap. It is to the credit of the minister in the verbatim that he did, in fact, go on to define himself and then return to Mrs. X's frame of reference communicating an awareness of and appreciation for her dismay.

It is this kind of empathic response that is the essential aspect of creative encounter. The minister's definition is the "Here I am," and his empathic response is his demonstration of his understanding of "There you are." It is in this sense that the "I sat where they sat" (Ezek. 3:15) takes on meaning, that "see things from other people's point of view" (Phil. 2:4 Phillips) is fleshed out in an incarnational sense. The initiative, as we have said, involves coming to the person(s) not only spatially, but also emotionally and spiritually. The conversation continues:

8. J.    Now, Adele; you know the preacher's seen messed up living rooms before.

9. A.    Yes, but . . . *(her voice trails off)*.

10. P.   Uh, you said that Martha was here; could she come visit with us?

11. A.   Well, yes. . . . She's doing her homework, and I'm sure she'd welcome any excuse to get out of that. . . . I just don't understand that child . . . not a thing like Sarah. . . . I'll go call her . . .

12. J.   *(As Adele gets up to leave the room.)* Now, Adele, she's doing all right. You'll just have to remember that they are different. *(To the minister.)* She worries a lot about Martha—too much, I think.

13. A.   *(Returning)* She'll be here in a minute. . . . That child! Reverend, what do you think about making a child do homework? With Martha, it's like pulling eye-teeth to get her to study . . .

14. P.   Well, it's hard to say. Children are different, that's for sure; I suppose we try too hard to press them to do what we want . . .

15. J.   My words exactly! She'll make it all right. . . . By the way, Reverend, how is the campaign for the new organ coming?

16. P.   Well, I'm glad you asked that. Seems that *(he explains the positive and negative aspects of the project.)*

In this segment of the conversation it becomes painfully clear that the minister either cannot or will not relate to these parishioners where they are. The lines of force in the family system are already becoming clear. The mother identifies herself as the "keeper of order and appropriate behavior"; the father is much more willing to "live and let live" and has no desire to wrestle with the differences and ambiguities. From Adele's perception, Sarah has responded appropriately, and she is frustrated that Martha does not follow the same pattern. Moreover, she is irritated that John does not help her, and she attempts to enlist the minister on her side.

An understanding of the most elementary aspects of family systems would be of value to the minister in taking personal as well as geographical initiative to come to parishioners. The critical response was 14 P. The first part is definition, and although it might be worded differently, at least it told them where he was. It was the generalization that followed which jettisoned his opportunity to encounter both John and Adele constructively. If, following the definition, he had said to Adele something like, "But it worries you when you think of what Martha is doing," he would have communicated his understanding of her viewpoint at a significant level. This kind of response makes for the reestablishing of broken relationships as Adele experiences someone who takes her seriously even though he does not agree. The encounter does not stop there, however. The minister is "for" all the family members, not simply Adele. Thus, whether or not John comments at this point, the minister turns to him with some such words as, "Yet, John, you're not sure but what Adele presses too hard at times." In this way the encounter includes both of them and the opportunity is provided for their dealing with those aspects in their relationship which have been barriers.

Unfortunately, as it was, the minister sided with one dimension of the power struggle and in so doing lost, at least temporarily, the opportunity to move toward reconciliation. John, in 16, was quick to seize this advantage and diverted the conversation to the campaign for the new organ, a diversion that the minister took without apparent question.

In regard to contract, Adele twice moves from "what" to "how." In reference to the room's disarray, she expressed uneasiness; in reference to Martha she expressed frustration and irritation. The minister responded to the former, as we have seen, but ignored the latter. Whether he was feeling somewhat anxious about John's position is not clear. In any event, he backs away from Adele's request. John, on the other hand, also expressed personal concern. In 12, the final statement is a "how" statement, i.e., "I wish Adele would ease up; her pressure on Martha upsets me." This, also, is ignored by the minister; and in J 15 the contract is broken by the question. Even so, this withdrawal by the minister is not necessarily the end of the matter. The feelings that have been repressed are still there, and in all likelihood he will have another opportunity to relate pastorally to this family. This factor is of considerable encouragement to ministers who realize either at the time or (as was the case for this person) in retrospect that an opportunity has been overlooked. The assurance that the opportunity will come again in all likelihood can make for more sensitive relationships. The conversation continues:

17. M.　　*(Entering)* Hello, Reverend Johnson. Good to see you.

18. P.　　Good to see you, too. How's the homework going?

19.M.  Not too hot; boy, they expect us to slave our lives away! Reverend, will you excuse me a minute? Daddy, I need some help with this trig problem . . .

20.J.  Okay. Maybe if I can't get it, the Reverend can give us a hand. *(They look at the problem as Adele and the minister sit in some uncertainty. In a very brief time the problem is solved.)* Martha, would you like to take a break and visit with us for a while?

21.M.  Yeah, how about me getting some Cokes
. . .

22.A.  I'll help you. . . . We also have Seven-Up, Reverend . . .

23.P.  Coke is fine . . . *(They leave)*

24.J.  Adele really does get up-tight. I wish she could roll with the punches a bit more, but
. . .

25.P.  Yeah, I know what you mean. Sometimes I think Shirley [his wife] rides the kids too hard . . .

26.J.  Yeah. . . . By the way, did you see that they're going to try to impeach Judge Williams?

Once again, the opportunities for pastoral care emerge in the family structure. At 24 John returns to the matter first introduced in 12. It is significant that in both instances he waits until Adele is out of the room to bring it up. And, again, the minister ignores the parishioner by commenting on his own situation. In the discussion of this pastoral call with colleagues, he indicated that at the time he was not at all conscious of his pulling back, but could see it clearly in retrospect. In the words of Revelation

3:20, when John opened the door, he had been unable or unwilling to come in. Some such response as "It really worries you and you aren't sure what you can do about it" could have been the means to stand with John in his struggle. When it is evident that the minister will not take his concern seriously, John diverts the conversation again. The visit continues:

| | | |
|---|---|---|
| 27. P. | | *(Takes Coke and cookies as Adele and Martha return.)* Thank you, this is great. How's school, Martha? |
| 28. M. | | The pits! I'd like to quit, but I can't! |
| 29. P. | | Driving you right up the wall . . . |
| 30. M. | | That's the living truth. The kids are creeps and the teachers are weird . . . |
| 31. A. | | Now, Martha . . . you've got some nice friends, and you like Miss Jones . . . |
| 32. M. | | Yeah, but . . . |
| 33. J. | | *(Interrupting)* Martha hasn't liked school since she put her foot in the first grade . . . |
| 34. A. | | If she'd just make up her mind that this is the thing to do . . . Sarah never had any problems with school, and . . . |
| 35. M. | | Mother, I'm not Sarah, and don't want to be; she does her thing and I do mine. . . . *(Pause)* Excuse me, Reverend, I'd better get back to my homework . . . |
| 36. P. | | Well, I can understand that. . . . I expect I'd better be going, also. *(Standing at the door.)* It's been good to visit with you all, and I look forward to seeing you in church on Sunday. |
| 37. J&A. | | Come back, any time. Always good to have you. |

In this final segment of the visit the minister, once again, had the opportunity to relate to these parishioners in a genuine encounter that could lead to more constructive relationships between them. This time the door was opened by Martha, who voiced some of her frustration and resentment at Adele for comparing her with her sister. In 35 at the pause he might have moved to her as he had to some extent in 29; but the moment passed, and he was silent.

We have reiterated that the parish minister is ordinarily not equipped to engage in family therapy and that is obviously true in this situation. Even so, an understanding of family structure at some level or other is crucial for effective family ministry. The saving feature of this pastoral visit was the minister's presenting it in a discussion with colleagues toward gaining new understanding of the opportunities for reconciliation. He saw, in retrospect, that although he had taken the initiative to come to these parishioners geographically, he had not done so personally. More poignantly, when they had covertly requested his help, he found himself unable to respond. Nevertheless, as a consequence of his peer discussion, he reached a new awareness of the ways he could be the means for facilitating more constructive and creative relationships in this family, and subsequent visits revealed the genuine progress he had made.

### B

We turn now from a situation where the minister had no prior knowledge of any tension or difficulty to one where the opposite is the case. In many instances, the minister knows or suspects that all is not well but has not been approached by the person or persons involved. Here, the implications of initiative and freedom are even more compelling. It is one thing to make a call and allow the person(s) freedom to move the conversation in any direction when there is no prior evidence of distress. It is another to initiate a call where the distress is evident and be willing for the parishioner to refuse to deal with the issue at hand. One factor helpful to the minister in such circumstances is the awareness that personal distresses fall generally into one of two categories. On the one hand, there is the whole range of difficulties that, however painful and destructive, carry little if any social stigma. These include such things as most physical illnesses, whether or not the person is hospitalized; losses suffered by the violence of nature such as tornado, fire, or flood; separations of the sort occasioned by a son or daughter going away to college or being sent overseas in military service; personal suffering, either emotional or physical, occasioned by forces over which the individual has little if any control. Usually, these kinds of situations are apparent in the fact that their existence is common knowledge, although this may not be the case.

On the other hand, there are those difficulties which carry not only their own inherent pain and distress but also the added burden or embarrassment of shame or guilt. These include such things as failures of all sorts, e.g., the failure of marriage, failure in business, failure in school; as well as circumstances that are perceived to have negative moral value such as unwanted pregnancy, attempted suicide, or various sorts of addiction, and so on. In addition, there are distresses that fall into one or the other category depending on the community and the mores. Distresses such as the birth of a retarded child, the occurrence of emotional illness, and various physical ailments, including venereal disease, may or may not carry a corresponding weight of personal disgrace that gives the individual the feeling of being cut off from the community. Where there is some sort of perceived social stigma, the persons involved tend to conceal the situation insofar as possible. Of course, some are so obvious that no such strategy is possible; even then, there may be a kind of general "ignoring" of the circumstance.[13]

Ordinarily it is easier for the parishioner to talk about the first category of distress than the second. Even so, there may be a reluctance to discuss either, and it is this reluctance that makes an understanding of the contract essential for effective pastoral care. Because the resistance is usually more evident in the second category, our exploration of such a pastoral call is undertaken in chapter 5 as the minister takes the initiative in going to see Mr. Howard, who is having difficulties with alcohol. The following verbatim illustrates the necessity for the pastor to be sensitive to resistance even when the distress is readily apparent. Unfortunately, an honest desire to be of help blinded this minister to the continued unwillingness of the patient to enter into a relationship with her. The call occurs in a hospital where the minister is participating in a clinical pastoral education program conducted by the hospital chaplain.

### Mrs. B

Mrs. B. is a 46-year-old married person admitted to the hospital for tests two days ago. She is scheduled for radical surgery tomorrow. She is well-groomed, looks younger than her 46 years, wears a wedding band and watch. No cards or flowers are visible in the room. (B = Mrs. B; M = Minister)

1. M.    Hello. I'm the chaplain on this section, one of the ministers here in the hospital. How are you today?

2. B.  Not so good.
3. M.  Oh, something bothering you?
4. B.  Yes, I have an operation coming up.
5. M.  Is it the thought of going on the table or what you expect after it?
6. B.  Both. *(Silence)* . . . But I guess it has to be done.
7. M.  But you're uneasy over it.
8. B.  Yes. *(Silence)*

Several issues emerge at the very outset of this conversation. In the first place, this minister missed the opportunity for a much more realistic definition of herself and why she was there in 1 M. She knew that Mrs. B. was scheduled for surgery, and her saying so when she introduced herself would have made the encounter much more realistic. Rather than "How are you today?" she could have followed her statement about who she was with something like, "I understand you are to have surgery, and I came to see if I could be of help." With that kind of honest word, Mrs. B. can accept the offer of the contract, or can immediately indicate that she does not wish to talk about the matter.

As it is, there is some uncertainty whether she wishes to discuss the surgery and her feelings about it. We have seen that a person begins to make the contract when the conversation turns from "what" to "how." In 2 B, she is clearly feeling oriented, and the minister's response in 3 M picks this up. The response in 4 B, however, is purely factual and strongly suggests that Mrs. B is probably not desirous of going any further. The probe at 5 M represents the minister's genuine willingness to be with her, but the silence at 6 B portrays reluctance. Just how long the silence lasted we do not know. It is likely that it was an uncomfortable time, and Mrs. B goes on to say that there is really nothing that can be done about the operation but have it. Again the minister presses her for feelings, and again her factual answer says loudly that she does not wish to discuss the matter. Once more there is silence.

In any pastoral conversation, the minister has a responsibility to prevent silences from becoming coercive. This is primarily true when the minister has taken the initiative in the call. Such a silence puts great pressure on the person to say something, and as such is a denial of the freedom not to open the door. If, on the other hand, the person has come to the minister either geographically or in an emotional sense by moving the conversation from fact to feeling, then the person has a right to silence when the minister has responded appropriately to what has been said. The rule of thumb, then, is that it is the minister's silence (that is, s/he has the responsibility to break it) if s/he has taken the initiative in coming to the parishioner and the parishioner has given no indication of wanting to establish a contract; on the other hand, it is the parishioner's silence (that is, the parishioner has the privilege either to remain silent or to speak) if s/he has begun to deal with personal feelings and the minister has responded appropriately to those feelings. In the latter situation the person may wish to muse over what has been said, and the silence can be fairly long. [14]

In the conversation with Mrs. B, dealing with the silence at 8 B is definitely the responsibility of the minister. Unfortunately, she continues to press Mrs. B to talk about her operation.

9. M.　　Your surgery is to be on the breast, is that right?

10. B.    Yes, I was to have a lump removed.

11. M.    You sound uncertain. *(I knew she was to have a radical breast surgery, but the nurse did not know whether Mrs. B knew.)*

12. B.    They are going to have to wait until they operate and then determine how far they have to go. They found malignancy.

13. M.    What you thought was going to be simple may turn out to be more extensive.

14. B.    Yes. *(Her eyes become moist.)*

15. M.    And it's scary.

16. B.    How about that! You see people walking in the street healthy as can be, it seems, and they may all be sick.

17. M.    There you were—healthy as can be just a while ago, but now, who knows?

18. B.    How about that! Who knows? That's me, all right.

19. M.    The uncertainty is kind of tough to take.

20. B.    It sure is. But I'll have to wait and see.

21. M.    But the possibilities make you uneasy.

22. B.    They sure so.

23. M.    *(At this point, I asked about her family, children, husband, etc. For some reason I felt that I needed more knowledge of her situation. As I look back, I believe she had terminated, and I was still trying to keep the conversation going. I asked about the time of the surgery hoping that we could continue, since it seemed to me she was really struggling with deep feelings.)*

24. B.    It's at eleven o'clock. So here I am.

25. M.    Wishing it could be otherwise.

26. B.    Yes. But I have to have it done.

27. M.   It needs to be done, but you wish it could be avoided.
28. B.   How about that. I just don't know. (*I could see a great deal of feeling in her face.*)
29. M.   Kind of works you up inside.
30. B.   It sure does. But what has to be, has to be.
31. M.   Yes, I know. But it is still tough.
32. B.   Yes, it sure is. And how about you, Chaplain, how are you doing?
33. M.   I'm fine. (*Pause*) Yes, actually, I'm feeling very good. (*I felt guilty about being able to say I felt well.*)
34. B.   Are you the chaplain here?
35. M.   There are several of us. I visit in this area. I try to see folks who are to have surgery. We try to be of help. But that's not always easy to do.
36. B.   I suppose not.
37. M.   I will be thinking about you and will see you after your operation.
38. B.   Please do.
39. M.   Good-bye for now.

It would be difficult to find an interview in which the minister so consistently ignored the parishioner's reluctance to talk about an obvious distress. Every statement of Mrs. B is evidence that there is no contract. All of her responses are factual, deal with solution insofar as she can envision it, and contain no words of "feeling" as would be the case had she desired to continue. In 23 M the chaplain calls attention to her perception of the situation, but is driven by the necessity to "minister" whether or not Mrs. B will open the door. Finally, in 32 Mrs. B seizes the nettle and overtly turns the focus of the conversation to the chaplain. This obviously is a much more polite way of saying: "Go away, Chaplain. I do not want to talk with you just now." But the intent is clear except to the minister.

A clue to the meaning behind the minister's inability to hear Mrs. B resisting the contract is seen in 35 M, where she laments that it is not always easy to be of help. In discussing the conversation in a later seminar, she became aware of the fact that this statement was actually a rebuke of Mrs. B, chiding her for not "being a better patient who would fill my needs to minister to her!" It was at that point in the seminar discussion that the meaning of initiative and freedom began to take on new significance for her in terms of the question, Whose needs are paramount in the interview? It is certain that in any true pastoral relationship, the needs of both persons are present and will be met to some extent or other. It is only when the needs of the minister take precedence over the needs of the parishioner that the positive values of the relationship deteriorate. Thus, in the conversation as recorded, the needs of the chaplain to minister to the patient transcended the patient's need to be left alone at the time, and the consequences were negative. Out of the seminar discussion came a new appreciation by the chaplain for the necessity that the person's freedom to open the door—or leave it closed—be maintained if the pastoral relationship is to be creative.

## C

There is one final word regarding the implications of initiative and freedom for the work of the minister. The two conversations recorded above deal either with persons in families or individuals in situations such as hospital confinement or other similar isolating circumstances. The principles are applicable in the wide varieties of personal and family life encountered by the minister.

By the same token, the minister often has an opportunity to work with groups of persons who may or may not be bound by blood or family ties. Here initiative is evident as the minister attempts to relate to the several members of the group in an appropriate fashion. It is the matter of freedom that is most often crucial. Many of the excesses associated with "sensitivity" groups which overlooked the person's need for various protective mechanisms at certain points could have been avoided if the concept of freedom had been operative. I have been appalled at the brutality often evidenced in the name of openness and honesty where persons were literally devastated by onslaughts in sensitivity groups, where the factor most lacking was sensitivity itself. Unfortunately, all too many of the leaders of such groups seemed to have little if any awareness of the consequences of the techniques and devices used to "open up" persons. Most apparent was the inability or refusal to deal with the pathology of sadism and masochism; tragically, in all too many instances these manifestations were praised rather than challenged. As a consequence, the genuinely positive value of group interaction has often been obscured by such practices, and persons who could truly benefit from the type of growth possible only in such a corporate setting have avoided or even attacked the notion of group growth itself.

It is encouraging to note that in recent times many who were negative if not hostile to group process as a means for human growth have changed their attitude as many of the earlier excesses have been set aside in favor of more creative encounter. It is my hope that an awareness of the meaning of initiative and freedom will further open the way for enabling persons to drop their facades, not because they are stripped away, but because the hiding is no longer needed in the experience of genuine encounter marked by acceptance and love.

## IV

In this chapter we have been considering the biblical theme "initiative and freedom" together with its implications for pastoral care and counseling. The context is the centrality of the reestablishing of broken relationships, the bringing back together of persons who are separated, isolated, and alone. We have seen the importance of the pastor taking the initiative in such endeavors, the searching for those who wander in loneliness or who are separated by barriers, in order to provide an invitation to communion. In like manner, we have seen the cruciality of maintaining the person's freedom so that the relationship when established can be genuine and meaningful.

Throughout, it has been evident that persons both long for such a relationship to overcome the isolation and aloneness, and draw back from it by reason of past experiences where closeness brought injury. Thus, the factor of fear assumes an increasing importance in an understanding of the meaning of pastoral care and counseling. It is to this that we turn in a consideration of the biblical theme "fear and faith."

# Chapter Three
## *Fear and Faith*

Throughout the discussion of "initiative and freedom," we noted that there is at one and the same time a desire for help and a resistance to being helped. Essentially, the resistance takes the form of a fear of being found, the word that marks Cain's agonizing cry, "whoever finds me will slay me" (Gen. 4:14). It is heard in the word of Ahab to Elijah, "Have you found me, O my enemy?" (I Kings 21:20), and it prompts the repeated rejection of Jesus which appears in the phrases, "go away," "leave us alone," "depart from me" (Luke 5:8, 8:37; and others), which essentially say, "do not find me."

Paradoxically, the term "fear" appears in two forms in the Bible. On the one hand it is the appropriate and proper attitude toward God, the "fear of the Lord" which is "wisdom" (Job 28:28) is "clean, enduring forever" (Ps. 19:9), is "the beginning of wisdom" (Ps. 111:10), is "to hate evil" (Prov. 8:13). In the Isaiah prophecy of the Messiah, we are reminded that "the Spirit of the Lord shall rest upon him, . . . the spirit of knowledge and the fear of the Lord. And his delight shall be in the fear of the Lord" (Isa. 11:2, 3). The "fear of the Lord" is a "treasure" (Isa. 33:6), and Jeremiah deplores the fact that the people "do not say in their hearts, 'Let us fear the Lord our God' " (5:24). The same notion runs all the way through the New Testament. The "unrighteous judge" in Jesus' parable is

quoted as saying, "I neither fear God nor regard man"
(Luke 18:4). Cornelius is described as "a devout man who
feared God with all his household" (Acts 10:2); and Paul,
in his sermon at Antioch of Pisidia, addresses the people
as "Brethren, sons of the family of Abraham, and those
among you that fear God, to us has been sent the message
of salvation" (Acts 13:26). The concept reaches a climax in
Revelation when the twenty-four elders worship God "for
rewarding thy servants, the prophets and saints, and
those who fear thy name, both small and great" (11:18).

Quite in contrast to this positive use of the term "fear"
is the tearing, agonizing, paralyzing fear that causes
persons to hide, to seek darkness, to cut themselves off
from the life-giving relationships so essential for their
being. It is to this kind of fear that we turn our attention in
the theme "fear and faith."

# I

The evidence of fear as the crucial characteristic of
wo/man is set forth clearly in the Yahwist account of the
Eden story. When the Lord God calls out to the man as he
walks in the Garden in the cool of the day, Adam's answer
is not primarily geographical but personal. "I heard the
sound of thee in the garden, and I was afraid, because I
was naked; and I hid myself" (Gen. 3:10). It is this
poignant statement which becomes the paradigm for
humankind from that point on. No longer are the man and
woman able to move freely into open relationships;
rather, driven by fear they search frantically for some
place to hide. So it is that wo/man, created for
relationships, turns his/her back on the one thing that is
essential for being. The terrible irony is that s/he does this

under the twisted notion that the hiding is essential to preserve life. Just here is adumbrated the meaning of Jesus' word, "For whoever would save his life will lose it, and whoever loses his life for my sake will find it" (Matt. 16:25; see also Mark 8:35; Luke 9:24).

From this point on, wherever we encounter "Adam," we are struck by the pervasive factor of fear and hiding. Sometimes the hiding takes the form of physical flight; at other times it is evidenced in a lie that is designed to obscure the reality of the situation; again it may emerge in a hypocritical gesture such as a bribe or flattery; from still another perspective it may manifest itself in hostility or violence. The forms are varied, but the purpose is always the same, i.e., to retreat behind a facade, to put on a mask, to erect some sort of wall or barrier, to banish or destroy, anything to find protection from a relationship that portends destruction.

To trace the manifestation of fear and the consequent hiding through the Bible would be to quote it practically *in toto*. The selective references set forth here simply highlight the pervasive presence of this basic characteristic of humankind.

We have already called attention to Cain's agonizing cry, "Whoever finds me will slay me" (Gen. 4:14), as the unique expression of Adam's response to the Lord God in the Garden. Abram's lie about his relationship to Sarai marks his fear of being "found," of being known as he is. (Gen. 12:12. Cf. the repetition of the same narrative in Genesis 20 and 26, Isaac and Rebekah being the subject in the latter.) Jacob flees from the presence of his father and his brother following the treacherous bargaining for the birthright and obtaining of Isaac's blessing. When he has maneuvered to take his possessions from Laban, he establishes the Mizpah agreement as a protecting barrier to any future attack by his father-in-law. And as he faces the prospect of being encountered by Esau at Seir, he prays fervently to God, "Deliver me, I pray, from the hand of Esau, for I fear him" (Gen. 32:11).[1]

Moving on, the cancerous presence of fear is seen in the return of Joseph's brothers to Egypt when they have found their money in the full sacks and have been required to bring Benjamin, "And the men were afraid because they were brought into Joseph's house" (Gen. 43:18). The lament of Cain is heard again in their supplication to Joseph after the death of Jacob, which follows their words, "It may be that Joseph will hate us and pay us back for all the evil which we did to him" (Gen. 50:15).

To paraphrase the Epistle to the Hebrews, "time would fail to tell of Moses, of Aaron, of Joshua and the Judges, of Saul and David and Solomon and all the rest." Over and over we read in one form or other, "I am afraid, and I am hiding, since whoever finds me will slay me."

As the New Testament opens an angel of the Lord appears to Zechariah, and he "was troubled when he saw him, and fear fell upon him" (Luke 1:11). So, also, Joseph, Mary, and the shepherds who watched "their flock by night" (Matt. 1:18-25; Luke 1:26-31; 2:8-14). Often it is recorded that the disciples were afraid, e.g., when they were experiencing the great storm at sea (Matt. 8:23-27); on the Mount of Transfiguration (Mark 9:2-8); as they followed Jesus toward Jerusalem after his words about the cross (Mark 10:32); and when "they all forsook him and fled" on the night in which he was betrayed (Mark 14:50; Matt. 26:26). In like fashion, they were terrified by the Resurrection, and the concluding words of the abortive end of Mark's Gospel read, "And they went out and fled from the tomb; for trembling and astonishment had come upon them; and they said nothing to any one, for they were afraid" (Mark 16:8).

In the Gospel narratives, fear is certainly not confined to the disciples. Herod is frightened by the news of the birth of a king of the Jews (Matt. 2:1 ff.). The Gerasenes asked Jesus to depart after the man named "Legion" was healed, "for they were seized with great fear" (Luke 8:37). The chief priests and Pharisees fear what will happen to them unless they can do Jesus to death (John 11:45, and others), and on the morning of the Resurrection when the angel appeared at the tomb, "for fear of him the guards trembled and became like dead men" (Matt. 28:4). In the Book of Acts a typical statement is found on the occasion of the death of Ananias, "And great fear came upon all who heard of it" (5:5). And John, in the vision that begins the Revelation, was terrified by the appearance of "one like a son of man" and "fell at his feet as though dead" (Rev. 1:12,17).

Set against this overwhelming presence of fear as the universal condition of wo/man is the corresponding word, "Do not be afraid." To thumb through a concordance is to become aware anew of the repetition of the phrases, "Fear not," "Be not afraid," or some variation on the theme such as that spoken by Jesus on the night of the Supper, "Let not your hearts be troubled" (John 14:1). From Genesis to Revelation, the reply to Adam's terror and Cain's anguished cry is the same, "You don't have to be afraid."

Significantly, this word comes whatever the nature and form of the fear. In many instances, the fear is born out of a sense of guilt, an awareness of failure, and an anticipation of painful retribution. On other occasions, the fear is that of the unknown or the awesome, the terror arising from the prospect of dealing with the unfamiliar. In any event, it always gives rise to hiding, to a distortion of reality, to a frantic effort toward some sort of defense or protection. And in every circumstance, the word is the same, "Fear not." Indeed, it is possible to say that the primary word of the Gospel, the Good News of God, is simply, "You no longer need to be afraid."

Nevertheless, the word is far from simple. Spoken by itself, it has no meaning; even more, such a word alone is not only a hollow mockery but a cruel disregard for the power of fear. So it is that throughout the biblical material this primary word of the Good News is always accompanied by the substantive reality without which it has no meaning. The person need not be afraid because something is happening that makes the fear no longer appropriate or necessary.

The most pervasive form of this substantive happening is found in the words, "I am with you" (*inter alia,* Gen. 26:24). In such a fashion the Lord God speaks to Abraham, to Isaac, and to Jacob. It is the word that is given to Moses in preparation for the deliverance of the children of Israel (Exod. 3:12). It is the sustaining presence that continually enables the prophets to bear witness to the righteousness of God. It is the meaning of the affirmation in Psalm 23, "Even though I walk through the valley of the shadow of death, I fear no evil; for thou art with me" (v.4). The word reaches its fulfillment in the coming of the Messiah, whose name is "Emmanuel," "God with us" (Matt. 1:23) and moves toward the "holy city" where "the dwelling of God is with men. He will dwell with them, and they shall be his people, and God himself will be with them" (Rev. 21:2, 3).

Ever and again, the primary word takes on other forms that bear specific relevance to the circumstance of the person who is afraid. To Abram, the Lord said, "Fear not, I am your shield; your reward shall be very great" (Gen.

15:1). To Hagar, the words come, "Fear not; for God has heard the voice of the lad where he is" (Gen. 21:17). Angels become the bearers of the word in the narratives of the Incarnation, specifically at the time of Jesus' birth and resurrection. At times, the variation of the basic theme is spoken by another person, e.g., the word of Joseph's steward to the brothers when they return to Egypt with the money and Benjamin, "Rest assured, do not be afraid; your God and the God of your father must have put treasure in your sacks for you" (Gen. 43:23). An example of this type in the New Testament is the word of Paul to the Philippian jailer who is on the verge of suicide, "Do not harm yourself, for we are all here" (Acts 16:28). In whatever form the word is spoken, it is "presence" that gives it substance, "I am with you," "We are here."

The tragic dimension is seen in that it is precisely "presence" that the person wracked by fear is driven to reject. For "presence" is judgment, the coming of that which is perceived as certain to destroy. Thus, Adam in the garden finds it impossible to believe that the Lord God calls to him in order to restore the broken relationship. Rather, he hears the searching as the prelude to the direst of consequences, and he is unable to face the reality of his situation.

Just here is set forth the crucial fact that all reconciliation involves both judgment and forgiveness, both truth and grace. The judgment is not condemnation, although it is experienced in that form (cf. John 3:17-21). Rather, in the biblical sense, it is the simple but profound word, "There you are," and " I am here." Only this realistic "finding" makes possible the experiencing of forgiveness. Apart from it, the word of grace is irrelevant, since the person always feels, "If they really know who I am (where I am) then they would not love me." By the same token, the word of truth, "There you are," apart from the word of grace, "I love you," is destructive. Only when the two are held together is the reconciliation effected. It is in this context that the prologue to the Gospel of John describes Christ as bringing grace and truth (John 1:14, 17).

Thus, in the biblical sense, the reconciling word is: "There you are. You do not need to be afraid. I am here, and I love you." The "There you are" and "here I am" compose the word of judgment; the "I love you" is the word of forgiveness.[2] The consequences of the deed remain, but transcending this is the incredible creativity of grace. In the garden the Lord God finds the man and his wife and makes for them "garments of skins" to clothe them (Gen. 4:15).

And so the stage is set. The search for Adam, and Adam's terror, which leads to hiding, is repeated over and over again as we noted in considering initiative and freedom. How is it possible for the response to be yes? Whence comes the courage to "open the door" (Rev. 3:20), to move out from behind the facades and hypocrisies that at one and the same time defend and bring death? The biblical answer is faith as seen in the paradigmatic words of Jesus to the disciples on the night in which he was betrayed, "Let not your hearts be troubled; believe in God, believe also in me" (John 14:1). But this faith is no cognitive construct; persons clutched by fear lose the power to think reasonably. Rather, the faith is essentially trust, the hesitant, fearful, tentative response to one who "having loved his own who were in the world, loved them to the end" (John 13:1). In sharpest fashion the bringing together of truth and grace, "There you are; I love you" is acted out at the Table. "One of you will betray me. . . . You will all fall away because of me this night" are the words that are spoken alongside of "This is my body which is broken for you" (Matt. 26:20-35; I Cor. 11:23-26).

Only the trust born of love can enable the person to drop the facades, to emerge from the deadly dividing walls of hostility (Eph. 2:14), to participate in the reestablishment of the broken relationships, to accept acceptance in the sure knowledge of not being acceptable, to say yes to the invitation to the communion that gives life. The struggle of faith is never easy, but it is possible. Fear is powerful, but trust born of love is even more powerful. "There is no fear in love, but perfect love casts out fear" (I John 4:18).

## II

We turn now to a consideration of the implications of the theme "fear and faith" for pastoral care and counseling. The most apparent factor is that the focus of the minister is always toward the reestablishing of the broken relationships through the primary words, "There you are" and "I love you." Said in that form, however, the words are meaningless. So it is that the minister struggles to understand the language of fear, of pain, of frustration, of anger, of bitterness, of resentment so that s/he may walk with the person through the twisted "valley of the shadow of death." By constant attention to the direct encounter with the parishioner the minister seeks to communicate, "I am with you."

In the process, the minister is acutely aware of how difficult it is for the parishioner to engage in such direct encounter, to "be found." This is true, even when the externals of the situation seem to imply that the conversation goes easily. However placid the exterior, the minister may be sure that within the parishioner there is a wretchedness, an anger, a fear, a resentment at having to be helped.[3]

Thus, the encounter is a struggle to find and to be found. No objective analysis of the situation will do, no gathering of data or prescribing of behavior which serve only to distract from the crucial effort to meet, to transcend the barriers, to enable the emergence of trust. It is in this sense that the good news is not only spoken but also done. It is the fleshing out of the word in the deed that provides opportunity for faith.

Finally, the minister is aware that if the encounter does not happen in the relationship with the parishioner, it is not likely to happen at all. It probably will not occur "out there" unless it is experienced "in here." Despite the fact that the broken relationships are always, by definition, bound up with persons who make up the parishioner's social environment, the separation is a function of the parishioner and in that sense is always present. Who s/he is in life, s/he is in the pastor's study. The attitudes, feelings and reactions are part of the person's patterns of relating, and are not abandoned at the door to be discussed with the minister in some objective fashion. Rather, in the encounter with the minister there is provided an opportunity for the person to relate in new ways, to respond more openly, not only to the minister but also to those "others" who make up his/her world.

This is a crucial point, one we need to keep ever in mind as we are becoming more aware of the intricacies of personal involvement, particularly in family systems. Pastoral care can never be optimally beneficial unless the pastor is conscious of the relational dimensions of the parishioner's life, and, as we noted in chapter 1, avoids falling into the trap of believing that the troubles are somehow "bound up in the person's skin." Having said that, however, it is just as essential that the person not be seen as simply a victim, helpless to deal with personal relationships unless other significant persons can also change to some extent or other. In a word, personal problems are always relationship oriented, and the primary relationships are certainly family. Even so, in the relationship between the minister and the parishioner, significant freedom can be achieved by each person even though other members of the family do not participate in the process. Only as the awareness of the tension between personal dependence and personal responsibility is kept in focus can pastoral care and counseling be truly effective.[4] Put in biblical terms, once the person experiences love, s/he is then able to love, and thus become a means for reconciliation with those most closely a part of his/her life.[5]

## III

In the interview reported below, the meaning of this process is demonstrated in some detail. The parishioner is a young businessman, married, with two small children. He had a fairly brilliant record in college and seemed on the way to a successful career in business. However, it turned out that despite his ability, he had trouble getting along with the office staff. The situation became so intolerable he resigned his position and took another job at a reduced salary. It was at this time he decided to seek help and came to his minister "to try to get some handles on why I always seem to foul everything up." Regular interviews were scheduled, and in the early sessions most of the conversation turned on a recounting of the difficulties. The minister attempted to listen as carefully as possible, sensing the deep hurt, bewilderment, and anger that seethed within the parishioner.

The present interview is approximately the fourteenth in the series that has stretched over some four months.[6] It is set forth here not because it was more significant than the other interviews, but because it illustrates so poignantly the implications of fear and faith for pastoral counseling. The excerpt is taken, with permission, from a tape recording, edited only to remove all identifying data. As was true in the previous chapter, the dots ( . . . ) do not indicate omission of words but signify a pause or trailing off of the voice. P = parishioner, and M = minister.

We pick up the conversation about fifteen minutes into the hour. The parishioner has been talking about how often he thinks of the right thing to say or do only after it is too late, and expresses the wish that he might be more aware of what is happening while it is happening rather than in painful retrospect. As he sees it, he tends to lose his capacity to function when caught in the give and take of business or similar discussions. There is a long pause on the tape, and then he continues,

1.P.     I seem to be *so* afraid of other people and their emotions; and so little feeling for myself . . . that it is difficult for me to be with people, to feel comfortable in any close relationship.

2.M.     Scared to death just to be there with them, face to face.

3.P.     Yes. What are they going to think of me?

4.M.     Yeah. So terribly vulnerable . . . (*Long pause*)

Here, the agony of being found is clearly seen. "Whoever finds me will slay me!" The minister does not interrupt the silence. When the parishioner has spoken and the minister has replied to the deep feelings expressed in words designed to say, "I am with you," then the parishioner has the right to continue speaking or to remain silent. After several minutes, the parishioner speaks:

5. P.   I guess it serves some need, but I'll be danged if I know what. It's almost as if I want them to say, "You're not OK!" [M: Hm.] . . . So I can say, "I'm sorry."

6. M.   And if I get you right, it's kind of baffling to you to think you might want some sort of condemnation.

7. P.   Uh–huh . . . As if I want them to validate my "not OK-ness" . . . and then I stand in wonder when they do . . .

8. M.   As though you set yourself up, and then think, "Why did you hit me? All I did was stand here with a sign saying, 'HIT ME,' and loan you the baseball bat . . . "

9. P.   Yeah. Get them to take a swing, since somehow I'll get some kick out of it or something . . .

10. M.   And yet still a puzzle to you. "How in the heck could I get to the place of wanting negative feedback?"

The minister resists the temptation to be diverted into a discussion of personality dynamics at 6 M. However interesting might be an exploration of the tendency toward inviting failure as a defense against failure ("If I had really tried, I would have succeeded") any such procedure would interrupt the encounter, which depends not on knowing why the parishioner is where he is, but rather on being with him now, whatever the reason for his predicament. The parishioner continues:

11. P.    And at the same time craving for someone to come up and say, "Gee, that was great; you're accredited . . . "

12. M.    Wanting it so badly . . . I almost get the feeling you're saying, "The only word I can believe is the negative, but I'd *sure like* to get the positive, even if I can only hear the negative."

13. P.    And I might even go so far as to hear it when it's not even there . . .

14. M.    Almost as though you made it up, read it into what they say, or don't say as the case may be . . .

15. P.    Yeah . . . my little brain tells me that they are after me out there, their emotional feeling about me is bad . . .

Here, again, is the wail of Cain, the projection of negativity on everyone "out there," the dreadful prospect of rejection. Just here the minister is aware of the fact that this feeling includes him, not simply those "out there." The tendency to believe that "here we are and you clearly trust me" is certainly an illusion. Thus, instead of moving the conversation to "out there," he stays with the parishioner, searching for him, "Adam, where are you?"

16. M.    Interesting to me that you used the adjective "little" with "brain," as though you're almost saying, "I really don't have much sense, and

|        |      | what sense I do have tells me these things . . . " |
|--------|------|----|
| 17.P.  |      | Sometimes I feel that way . . . |
| 18.M.  |      | The kind of "Not-OK" messages you were talking about awhile ago. |
| 19.P.  |      | Yes . . . And as I'm saying that, I get sort of tense, a sort of tenseness, like it hurts, a kind of tightening in my neck . . . |
| 20.M.  |      | Is it that you are tightening up in anticipation of being hit? |
| 21.P.  |      | Yeah. Giving *you* a big baseball bat . . . |
| 22.M.  |      | Yeah, saying, "Whop me!" And tense up and cringe, as though I am going to hit you . . . |
| 23.P.  |      | Yeah . . . Expecting it . . . |

The minister's comment on the use of "little" by the parishioner represents his attempt to respond to every signal that may give a clue to where he is. This reply carries no value judgment regarding the parishioner's capabilities. It is the plain and direct entering into the world of the person, a moving to stand with him in his wretched negative self-assessment. The temptation here, as in the interview with the family discussed in chapter 3, is to engage in reassurance. In this instance, such reassurance could be supported by data and evidence. "Of course you're not stupid; just look at your college marks and your IQ score!" Even with such substantive fact, however, the result is the same as when one attempts to guarantee the future ("everything will turn out all right"). The parishioner "knows" these facts, but they are meaningless to him. Thus, such a strategy is as much a rejection as facile words of comfort that have no tangible support. In each instance what is communicated is, "Don't tell me where you are; I *know* already where you are, and it is up to you to tell me you are there!" Clearly, this word makes impossible the encounter that, alone, can bring reconciliation and redemption in reestablishing the broken relationships.

The other side of such destructive reassurance is any and all manner of condemnation and coercion. In the interview, the minister might have been tempted to say: "Now you know better than that. Such a notion about people is ridiculous, and you ought to be ashamed of yourself for saying anything of the kind. What you need to do is develop a more realistic notion of the world, and the sooner you get started on it the better." This, like the reassurance, is also essentially destructive. Exhortation to the drowning man to remain on top of the water since it is much healthier than going under is factually true but not helpful. What is needed is not this comment on the obvious but someone who can come to him and sustain him until he can make it on his own.

As it was, the minister avoided both of these pitfalls. His word is simply, "There you are," or "Is this where you are?" As a consequence of such a word, the distress is no longer out there. Rather it comes to focus in the encounter, itself, and the parishioner notes that he is suddenly tense. Now, the two are no longer simply talking about the distressing situation; rather, they are experiencing it, and the way is open for a new relationship, even though it is, and will be, painful. The minister continues, stating simply his "Here I am" and "I'm for you and have no intention of punishing or hurting you."

24. M.     As a matter of fact, I haven't the vaguest desire to hit you . . .

| | | |
|---|---|---|
| 25.P. | But that doesn't make any difference . . . | |
| 26.M. | You expect it, anyhow . . . | |
| 27.P. | Yeah . . . *(Pause)* | |
| 28.M. | And my puzzlement at that point is, I get the feeling you're saying if I don't hit you, I'm not really relating to you in an honest fashion . . . that the only way I can be real is to hurt you . . . that if I'd really act on my genuine feelings, that's what I'd do . . . | |
| 29.P. | Yes. Apparently, I was feeling that and not really aware of it . . . | |
| 30.M. | So not fully in your consciousness, but your body saying, "All I can expect is a blow . . ." | |
| 31.P. | I expect that I've sort of made you into a father, I guess . . . and . . . well . . . | |
| 32.M. | And that's what you'd expect from a father. | |
| 33.P. | Uh-huh . . . *(Pause)* | |
| 34.M. | And not really know what to do with me when I don't bash you . . . | |
| 35.P. | Not sure at all . . . Well, not you, so much, as the image, I guess . . . | |
| 36.M. | Uh-huh. Know that I'm not really going to hit you, but expect it, anyhow . . . | |

The minister's definition of his actual feeling represents his purpose that the encounter be a genuine person-to-person experience. The parishioner has a right to know "who it is" that is "with me," not in any global sense, but in terms of what is happening right now. Personal definition (e.g., 24 M) ensures that the minister will not "disappear" as a person behind any kind of technique or method, will not remain aloof from the relationship, will not shield

himself from the risks of such close involvement.[7]
specifically, self-definition by the minister is indicated
when the parishioner asks for it, when it seems that the
parishioner's perception of him/her does not coincide with
his/her own, or when it seems that the parishioner's
understanding of data relevant to the situation is different
from that held by the minister. In each instance, the
definition is brief, factual, and honest; and having made it,
the minister returns to the person's perception to flesh out
the "here I am, there you are" aspects of the encounter,
which make possible the creative relationship.

At this point in the conversation, the minister's
perception of himself differs from that held by the
parishioner; his statement in 24 M is an affirmation of how
he sees himself. The progress of the relationship depends
on the minister's not entering into a debate on the matter.
Once it is said, that is sufficient, unless the parishioner
requests clarification. Thus, 26M returns to the parishioner's frame of reference. The minister's acceptance of the
parishioner does not in any sense depend on agreement;
on the contrary, it is paradoxically often true that in the
very act of disagreement the acceptance is experienced as
genuine and meaningful in that it transcends the ordinary
bases for affirmation of the person.[8]

Following the self-definition of the minister, the
parishioner states that he hears the words, but they have
no meaning. He is so locked into the attitude of expecting
punishment, he cannot move out of it. Thus, he finds it
quite difficult to allow the minister to be who he is. He
projects a role onto the minister which is contrary to the
minister's inner being. We recall Cain, who is certain that
when he is found he will be killed. Only tentatively is it
possible to conceive of any other attitude. This struggle is
clearly demonstrated as the parishioner continues:

37. P.    It's amazing . . . I was . . . I . . . kept "running out the door," saying "NO! NO! This isn't it." As if you were the father I couldn't let you accept me.

38. M.    Catch yourself resisting acceptance . . .

39. P.    Yeah . . . yeah . . . And the back of my neck is so *stiff*, so tense . . .

40. M.    Yeah . . . "What on earth would I do with genuine acceptance? Could I live with it?" You're not sure.

41. P.    Yeah. (*gulps*)

42. M.    You swallowed hard as if it sticks in your throat. Don't know what to do with me as an accepting person.

43. P.    (*Nervous laugh*) No idea in the least! None . . .

44. M.    So the other role may be painful, but you know what to do . . .

45. P.    Yeah . . .

46. M.    And to move out into the unfamiliar territory of being accepted really baffles you . . . What to do?

47. P.    Yeah . . .(*pause*) Feel sort of like crying. Such a hunger . . . need to have it . . .(*low voice*)

48. M.    And it's so hard to receive it . . .

49. P.    (*Very low voice*) Yeah . . . yeah . . . (*Long pause*) Here you are saying, "Truly, Bob, you are accepted," and you are . . . And I don't know what on earth to do with it . . . Except maybe run away . . . run away . . .

50. M.    Kind of a terrifying experience, hard for you even to stay here . . .

51. P.   It truly is . . . (*pause*) Oh, I won't really leave. I'll just build up a wall . . .

52. M.   To protect yourself . . .

53. P.   Yes . . . You want to accept me, and I'm paralyzed by my negative feelings. . . .

54. M.   Really puts you in a bind . . .

Here the struggle to open the door is seen in all its intensity. The parishioner longs for a positive relationship, yet fears it at the same time. The strain is evident not only in the words themselves, but in the physical tension (39 P), in the throat contraction (41 P), in the nervous laugh (43 P), and the faint voice (47 and 49 P). To say yes to the proffered relationship is to move into a world of openness, to forsake the constricting yet protecting barriers. Here is painful evidence of the incredible and wholly illogical process that makes the person "program" failure as a defense against the agony of failure. However bitter the rejections, there is the inner delusion that "they are not real, since I set them up; thus they can be explained." The paralyzing terror comes in the possibility that rejection may occur when there is no "programmed" reason, and that is perceived as too horrible to imagine.

This is a very crucial point in the relationship. For all manner of reasons, the minister might be tempted to "rescue" the parishioner, to engage in what could be called a kind of "pep talk," saying, "Of course you can trust me, just let yourself go." But, ironically, such words would be the undoing of the trustful relationship. What is at stake is the person's experiencing acceptance at the very point of his weakness, just when he finds himself longing to respond and drawing back at the same time. The comments in 48 M, 50 M, 52 M, and 54 M are spoken

to communicate a deep empathic awareness of the
parishioner's fear, to stand with him in the darkness, to
help bear the burden that is well nigh unbearable. These
responses represent the minister's saying: "Is this where
you are? Am I hearing you correctly? Am I truly
understanding your inner being?" This type of understanding is not objective or analytical; rather it is
intensely subjective in that it provides the means for
genuine encounter. That the encounter is happening is
seen in the next statement of the parishioner:

55. P.     Yeah . . . (*Long pause*) I'm not sure you
           accept me as a person with esteem, or do you
           accept me as a person with problems.
56. M.     Hard to sort it out, to know exactly what it
           means to you—or to me . . .
57. P.     Yeah . . .
58. M.     My genuine feeling is, "I'm for *you*, a fellow
           who's got a lot on the ball, and a fellow who's
           got a lot of problems . . . So, OK! There you
           are, and I'm for you!" . . . and yet when you
           hear me say it that way, hard not to feel,
           "yeah, but I'm not sure what to do with
           it . . ."

In 55 P, the parishioner says, in effect, "Who are you?"
In this particular situation he needs to check again on the
meaning of the relationship as determined by the person
with whom he is struggling. The definition of 58 M might
better have been spoken at 56 M. It is likely that the
minister was at this point so absorbed in the empathic
perception of what was happening between himself and
the parishioner that he was not aware of his own feelings
in any conceptual fashion. When he does respond, his

statement is simple and direct. It does not try to obscure the difficulties in a pseudo flattery, nor does it attempt to dwell on the difficulties at the expense of the positive dimensions of his perception. Having articulated his position in such a fashion, he returns to the parishioner, providing the freedom for him to accept or reject the definition depending on his own feelings at the time. The parishioner's reply demonstrates that he hears the words, but cannot honestly internalize them.

> 59. P. And you know, I heard "the fellow who has problems" louder than "the fellow who has a lot on the ball . . ."
>
> 60. M. At least this one sounded familiar . . .
>
> 61. P. Yeah . . . I heard it louder. Like a stereo system, one side turned up higher.
>
> 62. M. As though you catch yourself filtering me out, not going to let yourself listen to it . . .

When the parishioner notes his inability to pick up on the positive as well as the negative, the minister does not debate the point. However eager he is for the door to be opened, he will not force the issue. Significantly, the focus of the relationship becomes the parishioner's feelings about his own reaction to what the minister has said. This is a subtle point, one that is often overlooked. In the course of the conversation, the person may be verbalizing fear or anger or hopelessness or any other emotion. Then it may happen that s/he begins to experience a feeling about the feeling being discussed, e.g., shame, embarrassment, hesitance, or something of the sort. When this occurs, the focus of the conversation shifts to the "feeling behind the feeling" as representing where the person truly is at the moment. In 62 M the minister responds to such a circumstance wherein the parishioner longs to hear the positive, feels able to hear only the negative, and becomes aware of his resistance in the very process of dealing with the ambivalence of the situation. In this instance, the response provides a measure of freedom for the door to be opened just a bit wider.

63. P.   But it's nice to hear. I'd like for the record to get stuck just at that point and hear it over and over again, full volume.

64. M.   As you say that, I hear you almost allowing yourself to enjoy it, even though another part of you says, "No! No!" But it still sounds good.

65. P.   It's sort of like that part of me that might have something on the ball is a fantasy. The *REAL* Bob is the me with the problems . . .

66. M.   Yeah. So terribly difficult to live with the idea of having ability.

67. P.   Yeah. Like when you are a little boy, and make up games . . . Fantasy . . . You know it's not real . . .

68. M.   Make-believe. But when you get back to the real world, you're the negative Bob.

69. P.   Yes, There's the fantasy me, the good guy, the person with self-esteem, a nice fellow; and there's the other me, the *real* me, who's the goof-off, the clod, who makes mistakes . . .

70. M.   A real *bum*!

71. P.   Yeah . . . A *failure* . . . (*pause*) and that's kind of hard to swallow.

72. M.   Yeah. You really gag on that one . . .

It is here that the inner world is being revealed in all its terrible agony. It is as though the parishioner is saying (in 69 P): "Do you really want to know who I am? You've said you did, but do you, really? All right, I'll show you; and then you'll see how far wrong you were in saying that you have regard for me, that you accept me. Look!" The minister's response in 70 M is not a word of condemnation; rather it is a realistic word of accepting not the parishioner's self-assessment, but that this is the way he truly sees himself. He is aware of the fact that such a statement is at once a kind of belligerent defiance and a hope against hope that it may be possible to live out from under the heavy burden of hypocrisy. Put in other words, it is one means of testing the minister, of determining whether his former words are genuine or merely rhetoric. The words of confession are painful words, words that sear and tear. The remark in 72 M is the minister's way of saying, "You do not need to be afraid: I am with you . . . "

73. P.   The failure part keeps coming up. (*Pause*) And the strange thing is that my father never hit me; since I was about maybe four or five. . . . Maybe it would have been better if he had . . .

74. M.   Almost as if he had done that, you might have been able to deal with it . . . (*Long pause*)

75. P.   (*Low voice*) Maybe I kept waiting for it, and it never came.

76. M.   Seems to me you're saying that even though it didn't come, you were locked in to the notion, "that's the *real* response" whether or not it ever comes . . .

77. P.   Yeah . . . You know, objectively speaking,

|        |        | my father probably never saw me as a failure. And yet that image! |
|--------|--------|--------------------------------------------------------------------|
| 78.    | M.     | Crucial . . . and powerful . . . (*long pause*) |
| 79.    | P.     | Thinking about it makes my eyes water . . . (*soft voice*) |
| 80.    | M.     | Mine, too. |

This is a poignant segment of the emerging relationship of faith as trust. The parishioner has said how he sees himself, indicating that now at last he expects the blow will surely fall. It will, of course, not be a physical blow. Rather, it will be the crushing blow of rejection. "When they find me, they will kill me." "If you really knew who I was, you wouldn't love me."

Incredibly, from his point of view, the blow does not fall. He has bared himself, and he is alive. In this almost unbelievable experience, he discovers a perception of his father that had been obscured for years. It is still too incredible to be believed completely, but he is able to entertain the possibility. No longer locked into the conviction that the only honest response to him is punishment, he discovers that in all likelihood his image of his father is unrealistic. And for a moment, there are tears in his eyes as he contemplates the lost years, tears that find a genuine response in the sorrow of the minister as he participates in the experience.

The emergence of insight is a phenomenon often misunderstood in therapeutic practice. Here is clear illustration of the biblical principle discussed in chapter 1, which sees insight emerging as a consequence of experiencing forgiveness; it is an evidence of healing rather than that which produces healing. In the freedom that opens up to the person in the acceptance of being loved, it is possible to "see" that which has been there all the time but which was "edited out" as part of the deadly defense born of fear. As we saw, in the biblical sense, faith as trust leads to understanding, not the other way around. Throughout the Gospel narratives, it is recorded that the disciples did not understand what was happening, what the meaning of Christ's ministry of grace truly meant to them and to all persons. The experience of the cross and resurrection provided the freedom to "know" that which in one sense they had known all along but could not truly internalize.[9]

81. P.  There's a lot there, and it's so confused. Somewhere along the way I got fouled up . . . as a little child . . . I don't know . . .(*pause*). Thinking of it brought back tears . . . and I find it difficult to cry.

82. M.  Yet right now, your real feeling is to cry . . . (*pause*)

83. P.  Yeah . . . not as much as just a minute or so ago . . .

84. M.  Sort of got over it, couldn't really let yourself do it . . .

85. P.  I'm feeling quite a lot right now like a little boy . . . and there's a part of that that feels real good . . . Which kind of surprises me. I didn't realize that, but . . . uh, that little fellow got fouled up, somewhere. If I knew where, maybe I could correct it . . . (*pause*). How's all this sounding to you? My voice sounds quite far away to me, as though I'm back quite a few years.

Once again, the parishioner asks: "Who are you? What is happening to you as I say who I am?" This time the request takes the form of wanting some feedback, a word of reality as the minister sees it. The minister's definition serves not only as an affirmation of himself but also a "checkpoint" for the parishioner's pilgrimage through the strange land. It is a slow and tortuous journey, but it can be sustained if he is not alone. "Yea, though I walk through the valley of the shadow of death, I will fear no evil, for thou art with me" (Ps. 23:4 KJV).

| | | |
|---|---|---|
| 86. M. | | Actually, I didn't have any real conscious evaluative feelings of it, but when you raise it that way, . . . yes . . . it sounds soft, real, remote . . . (*pause*). Those are all the feelings I can come up with right now . . . I guess you're wondering if it sounded to me as it sounded to you . . . |
| 87. P. | | I guess the *real* me *is* kind of remote . . . [M:Uh-huh] somehow sort of covered by layers of not being OK, and all those experiences . . . (*pause*). Most of my tension is gone . . . |
| 88. M. | | You say that as though just suddenly you realize it . . . |

The full meaning of 87 P is perceived only when it is read in the light of 69 P. In the former, the "*real* me" is the "goof-off, the clod, who makes mistakes." Now, the "*real* me" is someone quite different, someone not immediately accessible, someone not at all well-known and yet someone quite positive. There is in the latter statement the evidence that in the parishioner as in all humankind is a genuine person struggling for life beneath and behind all the negative behaviors, the facades of hypocrisy, the rejection-producing attitudes and preju-

dices. In the biblical sense, the purpose of forgiveness is
to enable the person to be who s/he is, the restoration of
his/her real being through the dropping of the defenses,
through the opening of the door. In the creation story, it
is abundantly clear that Adam is a true person before the
Fall. Thus, sin is not of his essence, rather it is an
invasion, a distortion, and obscuring of his real self.[10]
When Christ, the "Second Adam" appears, he is truly
man, yet "without sin" (cf. *inter alia*, II Cor. 5:21).
Through the response of faith as trust, we are enabled to
become like him (cf. I John 3:2).

At this point in the counseling conversation, the
parishioner is suddenly conscious that he is no longer
tense. The easing of the strain has occurred not because of
any overt effort toward relaxation but by reason of the
experiencing of a relationship that is at one and the same
time realistic and accepting.

| | | |
|---|---|---|
| 89. P. | Yeah . . . There's something about that little fellow that was . . . good! |
| 90. M. | Sort of hard for you to understand it, but . . . not bad . . . |
| 91. P. | Yeah . . . Kind of the feeling that he might have been the fellow who was smarter, which raises all the questions of where this other me popped up . . . |
| 92. M. | Says to me, "You know, I wasn't always this kind of beaten, sorrowful, crushed, Bob . . . there may have been a little boy who laughed, made some mud pies, had a good time . . . " Not sure, but it's possible . . . |
| 93. P. | Yes . . . It surely seems so . . . |
| 94. M. | And you wonder where the "heavy" Bob came from . . . |

This is the second time the parishioner has made reference to a lack of understanding as to how he managed to get into the kind of defeatist attitude that has been so devastating. In 85 P he muses over the fact that maybe if he knew where he got fouled up he could correct it. There is in such a statement the strong temptation to begin an exploration of the past, to track the development from earliest childhood in order to discover some cause or reason for the present situation. All such efforts, however, move away from the person and the experiential relationship. It is certain that such a roundabout and indirect procedure can ultimately lead to a realistic relationship between pastor and parishioner; the sad fact is that all such searching, however well intentioned, tends to prolong the separation. The minister's response in 94 M betrays no subtle movement toward the past. The "wonder" is *now*, the only ground on which the encounter can occur. If the person does in fact move into a recounting of the past, whether it be the "past" of twenty minutes ago or the "past" of many years, the minister walks with him in the exploration. But the focus is always on the experience of the procedure, not the "data" that may or may not be turned up. Thus, as this parishioner speaks of the past, it is his "now" feeling about it that provides access to his inner being.

At a deeper level, there is seen here something of the biblical meaning of becoming as a "little child" as the access to the kingdom of God. There is no sense of "childishness," a characteristic often manifest in persons who have long since attained a chronological majority. The fact is that childishness is a rather common ploy for "hiding," for withdrawing from the kinds of relationships that could prolong life in a pseudo world of petulance, easily wounded feelings, pouting, and misery. In quite the opposite fashion, "childlikeness" marks that characteristic ability to trust, to wonder, to laugh, to cry without regard to the tyranny of the appropriate, without the necessity to assume a role, to play a part, to become hypocritical behind the mask of unreality. The parishioner experiences a "flash of recognition," a faint but real awareness that his present situation is not how he has always been. In this profound perception is the dawning of hope that since the state of wretchedness is not inherent but imposed there is at least the possibility that it need not always be present. In the exchanges that follow can be seen the miracle of new life.

95. P.   Yeah. I guess the real part was there at the time . . . but it is as if part of the stereo was turned up so high . . .

96. M.   and drowned out the other, since that's all you could hear . . . (*pause*)

97. P.   You said you accepted me, and I didn't know how to respond . . . to let you . . . And yet I guess I have . . .

98. M.   Just did it without knowing it . . .

99. P.   Yeah . . .

100. M.   I'm aware that you are smiling again . . .

101. P.   And I find myself sharing something with you that I haven't even shared with myself.

102. M.   Sort of amazing to you . . .

The meaningful statement here is 97 P. There is a mystery in the emergence of faith. It cannot be programmed, nor can it be forced. At one and the same time it "happens," and the person participates in the "happening." It is a genuine response to love in the experiencing of the relationship which is trustworthy. It is in no sense a decision in the ordinary meaning of that term although it becomes the basis for decisions of all sorts. It is for this reason that an appeal to the will is doomed to failure even though the person may engage in some sort of volitional activity. The fact is that the will is in bondage (Rom. 7:15-24), and is released only in the experiencing of forgiveness and reconciliation on the basis of which the person is able to decide (Rom. 8:1, 2).

In the biblical sense, all the verbs that relate to this type of liberating experience are passive. "We are saved," "we are reconciled," "we are redeemed," "we are transformed" give eloquent testimony to the fact that something happens to us. Although the verbs are passive, the person is never passive, as though something happens apart from his/her participation. Thus we can properly speak of faith as the response of trust to love, and know that in a realistic sense the person has freedom not to say yes in the paralyzing agony of fear. The forgiveness may have to come "seventy times seven" times (Matt. 18:22), but that is no matter for the mark of love is that it "never ends" (I Cor. 13:8). While the old Calvinistic term "irresistible grace" has often been misused to make for the dehumanizing of persons (i.e., puppets with no freedom), it contains a basic truth when set in the context of the emergence of faith as trust. The conscious awareness of faith at a cognitive level comes in retrospect, as illustrated in 97 P.[11] In the light of the new freedom, the parishioner is able to experience aspects of himself long submerged under the deadly shell of hiding as stated in 95 P. The tenseness is gone, and he is smiling (100 M) as he realizes that in this relationship he is free to become "himself" in a significant way.

103.P.  Feels kind of tender . . .[M: Uh-huh] (*pause*) . . . The other me wants to say it's not nice; but it feels good . . .
104.M.  Right now not quite as vulnerable to the "other me." You know the message, and yet have the feeling, "I don't necessarily have to believe it right now. I can believe what I really feel, and that's good."
105.P.  Yeah. I'm going to walk around the rest of the day feeling "GREAT!" "GOOD!"
106.M.  Yes . . .
107.P.  Now, why can't I do this with people outside?
108.M.  When it seems so natural and so good in here . . .
109.P.  Yeah . . . (*pause*) Our time's up . . .
110.M.  Yeah . . . See you next week . . .

In the concluding minutes of the conversation the parishioner is aware of the "old me" tugging at him, the old fears that die so slowly. Moreover, he has real uncertainty of being able to live "out there at the same open level, to face the environment that hasn't changed. Here, the minister makes no attempt to bolster the gains by some such word as: "Why, sure you can. You did it here, now just go to it out there." He knows, and the parishioner knows, that, following the Mount of Transfiguration experience, the wretched world of harsh and tearing events can produce all manner of doubt and despair. There is, therefore, no effort to emphasize the positive nature of the experience of freedom. So, the end of the hour comes, and they separate. They will meet again; but they will never be the same again. In this experience both have gained a new appreciation of the power of love to produce faith that overcomes and banishes fear.

## IV

In introducing the pastoral conversation, I called attention to the fact that this particular interview was included in the discussion not because it was more significant than any other in the series, but because it illustrated in graphic fashion certain of the concepts that had been discussed. I return to that point now, first of all to underscore it, and second to draw more generalized implications than were possible in discussing the segments of the relationship.

Faith is a process, never a static or fixed point. Despite certain "high moments" in a pastoral relationship as that which occurred in the transcribed conversation, such times are no more or less important than every other moment along the continuum of life. This awareness is crucial for any pastor lest s/he tend to become discouraged because there seems to be no "turning." In such a circumstance, s/he is likely to fall into one of two traps. On the one hand, s/he may tend to press too hard, to attempt to force some overt transformation, to squeeze the person into a desired behavior. I often think of a simile which is ridiculous but which is tragically appropriate, namely the act of tugging on a tender growing plant to hasten its progress only to pull the roots out of the ground and set the whole process back. The other trap, of course, is to give up, to reach the conclusion that since "nothing is happening," there is no need to continue. It is true that any minister may reach an impasse beyond which s/he cannot go; but this is a function of his/her own limitations and not inherent in the healing power of love. At such a time the competent minister does not give up on the person, but recognizes that s/he is not able to be the channel of grace that will bring life. Thus s/he makes every effort to enable the person to enter into a relationship with someone who can do so. [12]

In the biblical narrative, a ready illustration of this process point can be seen in the story of Simon Peter. Through the years we have regarded the Caesarea Philippi confession, "Thou art the Christ" (Matt. 16:16; Mark 8:29; Luke 9:20), as a high point in his relationship with Jesus, as, indeed, it is. Nevertheless, it is clear that this confession has no meaning apart from the "leaving of the nets" many months before. It is significant that Jesus did not raise the question "Who do you say that I am?" during that earlier encounter. It is tragic when we are tempted by the very best of motives to force the person to make what seems to us to be a desirable response long before it is appropriate to the person. Little by little, in the association with Jesus, Peter came to the point where the great confession gave evidence to the meaningful relationship that had been developing, a relationship made possible by Jesus' patient willingness that it proceed at its own pace.

From still another perspective, different from the tendency to become impatient or discouraged when no overt turning appears, is the temptation to invest such a turning with too great a significance. Few ministers have not felt a "now, at last" sense of relief when a parishioner says or does that which is perceived as a real step forward. No matter how genuine the rejoicing, the danger lies in the possible obscuring of the fact that though the battle has been won the war is far from over.

There is no place for resting on laurels in the sense of

believing that the struggle is past. In reality such a genuine turning may open the way to even darker moments as the person begins overtly to grope his/her way into new patterns of life. Such was certainly the situation of the parishioner whose conversation we have examined. In the weeks that followed, there were times when the blackness of doubt and despair seemed almost overwhelming. The fact is, however, that through the continued relationship with the minister, which lasted for quite awhile, he was able not only to work through the obstacles which continued to impede him, but reach the point where he could draw on the life-giving sources of the community of faith apart from the atypical regularly scheduled sessions with the minister.

Nothing could be clearer in the biblical narrative than that the progress of faith is jagged and uneven. The ninth chapter of Luke, which records the Caesarea Philippi confession and the Mount of Transfiguration experience, sets forth five "vignettes" that help us understand how long was the road of faith for the disciples. Peter wishes to stay on the mountain and avoid having to deal with the harsh world below; the Nine are unable to heal the convulsive child by reason of their lack of faith; the Twelve argue over who among them is the greatest; John rejects a man who is not "with us"; and James and John long to call down fire from heaven to consume the Samaritans who would not receive them. Much later, on the night in which Jesus was betrayed, they all forsook him and fled; and Simon Peter, who made the great confession, denied thrice that he knew him.

Only an awareness of faith as process that continually struggles with doubt and fear can enable the minister to respond to the person where s/he is at any given moment in the sure conviction that this moment is ultimately the most crucial since it is the only point available for encounter. The goal, then, becomes not some fixed destination, but the capacity to live in an openness which requires fewer facades and in which the person is able to meet any situation creatively (Phil. 4:13) because of the faith which is born of love and which overcomes fear. It is in this sense that the statement in I John takes on meaning: "and this is the victory that overcomes the world, our faith" (5:4).

# Chapter Four
## *Conformity and Rebellion*

We looked first at "initiative and freedom," and then at "fear and faith" as biblical themes that provide an understanding for the work of the pastor as counselor, and we saw that each involved the other at every point. So we turn to "conformity and rebellion" with the awareness that this dimension has already entered into the discussion. Our purpose here, as in exploring each of the themes, is to examine the process of pastoral counseling from first one perspective and then another in order that the whole may be seen in a clearer light.

## I

In the biblical narratives, conformity and rebellion are the two primary forms of hiding, of turning away from openness and constructive relationships. In each instance, the person attempts to conceal a part of his/her being, to present a facade that obscures his/her wholeness, to distort the reality of his/her response to others. Although either conformity or rebellion tends to become the general characteristic of a person's stance toward life, neither is ever present without the other. Beneath the external acquiescence to expectations and demands is rebellion, which can explode with great intensity. In like manner, beneath overt rebellion is an urge to comply.

These two characteristic responses stand out most clearly in the accounts of siblings. Beginning with the story of Cain and Abel and moving through the whole sweep of the Bible, the older sibling tends to develop the role of the conformist, and the younger, the rebel. Over and over the theme emerges with different participants and in different situations but always basically a repetition of the format set forth in the Genesis accounts.

We begin with the narrative of Cain and Abel in Genesis 4, and our focus here is on the first type or conforming sibling, since the story is essentially about Cain.[1] The bare facts are simple enough. Cain is a tiller of the ground, Abel a herdsman (v. 2). Each brings an offering to the Lord (vv. 3, 4). We are not told the occasion for the offering, what it meant to them, or why they brought it. For reasons that are not given, Abel's offering is accepted, Cain's is not (vv. 4, 5). Cain is infuriated by this turn of events and does not reply to the Lord's offer of help and support (vv. 5-7). Rather, in his wrath he kills Abel, lies to the Lord God, and experiences the same separation and isolation that marked the consequences of Adam and Eve's refusal to be that which they truly were (vv. 8-16).

Although the story is told in briefest form, it contains a profound wealth of meaning.[2] The first-type person sees acceptance as dependent on acceptable behavior: "They love me when I do what they want, and if I do not do what they want, they do not love me." Thus, when Cain's offering is not accepted, he feels that he is rejected as a person. He is angry and cannot rejoice in the success of his brother.[3] Rather, in a typical first-type reaction, his emotions, which have been pent up within, emerge with a fury that leads to destruction. His undoing is that he is unable to deal with failure. In the word of the Lord God, spoken to him as his anger is manifest, there is the clear delineation of the first-type response. As long as things go well, he has no problem; but when he fails, then his world tumbles in. It is just at this latter point that he has opportunity to move toward life or death (Gen. 4:7). God's coming to him is, as we saw in chapter 2, the taking of initiative in a manifestation of love and grace precisely at the point of his failure and anger. It is a word that says: "The offering was not acceptable, but you are! I am here out of a concern for you." Just here, another characteristic of the first type is revealed, namely, he cannot receive a gift. Locked in to the notion that he earns approval, he has no recourse as he sees it but to kill his brother in the irrational and futile attempt to be rid of this one whose acceptance has served to make him so agonizingly aware of his own failure.

When next the Lord God speaks to him, his word is, "Where is . . . your brother?" (Gen. 4:9). This word, along with the primary word to Adam—"Where are you?"—is the word of judgment and of grace. Where the person is always involves his/her relationship with his/her brother/sister. Thus, the consequences of the hiding, begun in the garden, are seen now in all their deadly dimensions. Cain lies in his response, and attempts to divert the conversation by the use of the term "keeper" (Gen. 4:9). Of course, he is not his brother's keeper. Persons "keep" animals, not their brothers. Nowhere in all the biblical narrative is there the notion that anyone is his brother's keeper; rather he is his brother.[4] Now Cain's failure is complete. His inner anger has literally exploded and destroyed his mechanisms for hiding. The conformist who tries to win approval by doing that which is expected now has become the rebel who destroys all around him. The miracle is that in the midst of the terrible consequences, the word of grace remains. For the Lord put a mark on Cain as evidence of his presence and sustaining power (Gen. 4:15).

By far the clearest counterpart to Cain is the elder brother in the parable of Jesus recorded in Luke 15:11-32. He devotes himself to complying with the wishes of the father ("I never disobeyed your command," v. 29) in the expectation that this behavior is required to win the father's love. He is infuriated when he discovers that the prodigal is being received in the house, and protests that the father never gave him so much as a kid to make merry with his friends (vv. 28-30). In his resentment he is blinded to the fact that the father gave him his share of the inheritance just as he had done to the prodigal (v. 12). He is not able to receive a gift, either his share of the property or, more poignantly, the gift of grace evidenced in the father's coming out to entreat him and invite him into the feast of celebration (v. 28). Driven by rage, he lashes out at the father and his brother, and as the story ends we are not at all sure whether he ever came into the house or not (vv. 28-32).

Between the story of Cain and the story of the elder brother, the theme of the first type emerges in varieties of forms but always with the same pattern. Not all the aspects are specifically set forth in each instance, but the central thrust is always there. Thus, first-born Ishmael, a shadowy figure at best, is pictured as one who is resentful and vengeful against Isaac and all his descendents. "He shall be a wild ass of a man, his hand against every man and every man's hand against him; and he shall dwell over against all his kinsmen (Gen. 16:12).[5] In similar fashion, first-born Esau longs to gain his father's favor by doing that which he perceives to be acceptable. "So when Esau saw that the Canaanite women did not please Isaac his father, Esau went to Ishmael and took to wife . . . Mahalath" (Gen. 28:8, 9). Moreover, Esau "hated Jacob because of the blessing with which his father had blessed him, and Esau said to himself . . . 'I will kill my brother Jacob' " (Gen. 27:41).

The brothers of Joseph form a composite first type even though, of course, each has his own identity. They are resentful of the favors shown Joseph by Jacob, and as they went to pasture with their father's flock ("these many years I have served you") they saw Joseph coming and said, "Let us kill him and throw him into one of the pits" (Gen. 37:20). In the story of Aaron and Moses, the time comes when Aaron longs to please the children of Israel and to supplant his younger brother, Moses, i.e., in effect to kill him. So it is that he aids and abets the scheme to fashion a golden calf for worship and sacrifice (Exod. 32:1 ff.). The list goes on and on.

In summary, the characteristics of the first type are clear. His/her tendency is to hide behind behavior that is perceived as acceptable, to do the right thing, to conform to external demands as a means for gaining love and favor. S/he feels rejected when what s/he does is not deemed appropriate, and resists letting his/her true self be known, since "if they knew who I was, they wouldn't love me." S/he finds it difficult to deal with failure, because to fail is to be found out, and thus not loved. S/he is aggrieved by favors granted others, and particularly the second-type sibling. S/he tends to suppress his/her inner feelings of resentment and rage since they are seen as unacceptable; and when these deep feelings do erupt, they do so with violence and often murderous destruction. S/he finds it difficult to accept a gift both by reason of the need to earn acceptance and by reason of feeling basically unworthy of the gift. In the crises of life, s/he either redoubles his/her efforts toward buying favors or lashes out in irrational and self-defeating behavior, which destroys his/her world of pseudo security. Although s/he hears the word of grace, s/he finds it incredibly difficult to respond to love.[6]

Having looked at the typical conformist pattern of hiding, we turn to the second type, or rebel. Only the barest rudiments appear in the Cain-Abel story. All we know about Abel is that his offering is acceptable and as the story ends he is in favor with the Lord God. Anything else is speculation, other than the characteristic experience of favor enjoyed by the second type, which becomes the occasion for rage and destruction on the part of the elder brother. However, the Bible is quite consistent in its portrayal of the typical second type, and while it would be inappropriate to read data back into the Abel material, there can be no doubt about the second-brother characteristics from a scriptural point of view.

Here, as above, we move to the parable of Jesus in Luke 15 for the clearest statement of the second-type theme. The prodigal, rather than seeking to gain acceptance by acceptable behavior, tends to be a rebel. He demands his share of the inheritance (Luke 11:12) and turns his back on the accepted and expected patterns of behavior. Within a short while, he has left home, and his way of life is a far cry from that of the brother "who never disobeyed your command." For a time all goes well, but the inevitable reversal sets in (Luke 15:14). Having burned his bridges behind him, he cannot go back, and he struggles with new and devastating circumstances (Luke 15:15, 16). Finally driven by despair, he stumbles home, no longer the rebel. His prepared appeal to the father is that he be made into a servant, that he be compelled to obey, to conform (Luke 15:18, 19). But when the father speaks to him, his word is a word of grace and forgiveness, just as it was to the elder brother (Luke 15:22-24). And as the story ends, he is in the father's house enjoying the things that might have been his all along (Luke 15:24).

As was the case of the first type, these characteristics appear over and over in the biblical narrative. Isaac, like Esau, is a somewhat indistinct character; nevertheless, although younger, he is the one who occupies the line of direct succession to Abraham. Jacob's rebellion is clear.[7] He tricks Esau out of his birthright and obtains Isaac's blessing under false pretenses. As a consequence he leaves home and, after the experiences at Haran, encounters God at Jabbok where he becomes Israel (Gen. 25–33). Joseph from an early age is pictured as arrogant and irritating. In due course he is sold into Egypt by the brothers. There he comes into favor, and as the story ends, he is his brothers' benefactor (Gen. 37–50). Moses, the younger brother of Aaron, flees to the land of Midian after killing the Egyptian, only to meet Yahweh in the burning bush and thereby become the deliverer of the people in the Exodus (Exodus 2 ff.). As before, the list runs on.

In summary, the second type tends to hide behind behavior that is atypical or destructive, to rebel against the external demands as a means for gaining recognition. "If I were simply myself, they would never know that I exist." The rebellious activities, however self-defeating, do enable him/her to make his/her mark, in contrast to the first type, who attempts to win recognition and acceptance by appropriate behavior. His/her behavior inevitably leads to distress, and the separation is accentuated by repeated aggression and withdrawal. At some point s/he leaves "home" and goes to a "far country." S/he longs for acceptance, but fears it since it seems to imply a loss of identity. S/he is terrified by loneliness but sees no prospect of being related at a meaningful level since such a relationship seems to imply a denial of being. S/he finds it hard to deal with success and often snatches defeat from the very jaws of victory. Accordingly, it is also difficult for him/her to experience forgiveness and grace. Nevertheless, when s/he is driven into abject despair, s/he discovers to his/her amazement that the consequences are life, not death. And in an unexpected reversal of circumstance, at the end it is s/he and not the conforming sibling who occupies the favored position.[8]

Looked at as a whole, the characteristics of the conformist and the rebel, however different in externals, stem from the same desire to hide. Both are alike in their resistance to being found, to being related, to being forgiven, to being loved. And each suffers the consequence of his/her pattern of behavior in isolation, loneliness, and death unless and until s/he is enabled to experience acceptance by grace through faith.

# II

We turn now to a consideration of the implications for pastoral counseling inherent in the first- and second-type sibling. The primary factor is that in the reestablishing of the broken relationships, an awareness of the strategy or ploy utilized by the person for hiding can make the minister more sensitive to the subtleties of facades and behaviors that at one and the same time invite and block open encounter. Obviously, this does not mean that the minister will spend time attempting to categorize the person, a sort of "Now let me see, is this parishioner a first or a second type?" Rather, it implies an increasing capacity to be aware of the patterns of response and to evaluate at a critical level his/her own reaction to the patterns.

The bondage of the first-type person is seen primarily in the necessity to gain approval by doing the appropriate or acceptable thing, as we have noted. Carried to an extreme, this characteristic manifests itself in rigidity, in legalistic compulsivity, and in the inability to tolerate deviation. Inevitably, these ploys and responses are brought into the counseling session. The most apparent evidence of the first-type response is the parishioner who consciously strives to please the minister by saying or doing what s/he believes the minister wishes. Such a person tends to have a kind of built-in "radar" capable of picking up the subtle expectations that the pastor brings to the situation. Not wanting to incur the minister's disapproval, this person may refrain from introducing into the conversation those aspects of her/himself which are perceived as unacceptable.

It is just here that the minister may stumble into a deadly trap. For when any negative behaviors or feelings are revealed, s/he may find her/himself drawn toward some kind of statement designed to excuse or reassure. Unless s/he is aware of the issues involved, his/her first reaction is that here is a person who has a record of success and who seems to be overreacting to some experience that did not measure up. In that case, his/her response would be something like: "There, there, now; to be sure you didn't do as well as you wished, but remember the many times when you have succeeded. I am sure that this is just a temporary setback, and you'll find tomorrow much brighter."

The cruel fact is that first-type people have suffered from being excused and thus denied the creative, although painful, experience of being forgiven. In such a circumstance, the opportunity to deal constructively with failure is lost since the failure is minimized or ignored. Yet deep within, the person knows full well the shortcomings of the act or attitude. And while, for the moment, the relief of being excused seems pleasant, it results in the far more agonizing consequence of "once they truly find out, they will not love me." It is just here that the basic difference between excusing and forgiving is seen in stark clarity. To excuse is to fail to take seriously the facts, to say, in effect: "It doesn't really matter what you did. I choose to ignore you and the consequences." To forgive, on the other hand, is to take the facts quite seriously, to say, in effect: "What you did was destructive, and its consequences are still to be borne. Because I love you, I want to help bear the burden with you, for I take you quite seriously, and who you are means more to me than what you did." In biblical terms, this means taking sin seriously and understanding that judgment as "truth," i.e., dealing realistically with the person, is essential for reconciliation and restoration.

In this light, the factor "There you are" is crucial for effective pastoral care and counseling of the first-type person. To be sure, the "I love you" must always be said in both word and deed; but if it is not said in the realistic context of "there you are," it is always perceived as irrelevant. Only as the first type experiences acceptance in the presence of failure is there possible any reconciliation and realistic reestablishment of the broken relationships.

At a deeper and more subtle level, the same necessity for realistic recognition of behavior is essential when it manifests itself in legalistic conformity. Because the legalistic first-type person is often technically "right," it may become more difficult to engage in a creative encounter that at one and the same time recognizes the destructiveness of the rigidity and yet communicates love for the person. In the parable of the two sons in Luke 15, many ministers and church members tend to feel a certain affinity with the older brother, an affinity that may take the form of concluding at some level or other that "after all, he did have a point; he had been at home working rather than squandering the family money, and he can be excused for being irritated with the lavish treatment given to the younger." As long as such a feeling prevails, the chances for reconciliation are small.[9]

Most poignant of all in pastoral counseling with first-type persons is the minister's hesitancy to deal overtly with what appears to be a "right is right" position for fear of being wrong her/himself. First-type persons tend to place blame outside themselves. "If this or that circumstance were different, or if this or that person were to change, then all would be well with me." There is usually enough truth in the statement to cause the minister to pull back from realistic encounter lest s/he be found in error. Thus the relationship suffers, as there is no genuine word of "There you are!"

Turning to the implications for second-type persons, the bondage lies in the necessity to gain attention by atypical and often destructive behavior. These characteristics are evident not only in the ordinary course of life, but also in the counseling session itself. The person may be late for appointments, make demands, and in various ways act in a thoughtless or irresponsible fashion in relationship with the minister. Thus, in direct contrast with the minister's tendency to excuse and reassure the first-type person, s/he may find her/himself irritated by and resentful of the behavior of the second type. The "there you are" may come readily enough; it is the "I love you" that is much more difficult. The tendency is to scold or exhort in some fashion or other. Paradoxically, such chastisement actually breeds more of the very behavior that it is designed to curb. The inner, and often unrecognized, feeling on the part of the second type is, "Well, at least s/he knows I am here." Just as the first type has difficulty dealing with failure, the second type has difficulty in dealing with success. When an appropriately cooperative activity is performed, the response is likely to be that it is ignored, or the person is told, in effect: "See there, you did it just fine; now why haven't you been doing that all along? I shall certainly expect a better performance from you in the future."

It is the perceived difficulty of dealing with success that often tends to make the second type avoid constructive activities. The overt complaint may be a self-depreciation, "I'm sure I couldn't do that; see how often I have failed before?" Underlying such statements is the gnawing anxiety that if the task is done—and done well—the consequent expectations would be too great to bear. Only as the minister is able to affirm the person with the possibility of either success or failure is reconciliation likely to be effected. The "I love you" is spoken without a pained "What, again?" in the event of failure, or a "See there, I told you so, now do better," in the event of success.

Perhaps the most pervasive ploy of the second-type person is a refusal to see her/himself as a person of genuine value. S/he may attempt to manipulate the minister into taking over his/her life, to make suggestions, to give advice, to assume responsibility for his/her behavior. It is noteworthy that in the story of the two sons, the younger determines to "instruct" the father regarding the treatment he should be accorded. "Treat me as one of your hired servants" (Luke 15:19). The possibility of reconciliation, however, rests on the fact that the father relates to him realistically, saying, in effect: "No, you are not a hired servant; you are a son! Come into the house." Thus, it is the minister's refusal to acquiesce to requests that s/he now assume charge of the parishioner's life that provides the most eloquent affirmation of worth for the person. It is a powerful way of saying, "I stand with you, not instead of you, and together we experience the strength that enables us to live creatively as persons." The person is thereby forgiven, rather than condemned or excused.

From the perspective of family systems the second-type child is often seen as the "problem" child. Many parents are puzzled and frustrated by his/her behavior and attitude when compared with the first type.[10] A typical expression is, "I just can't see how two children growing up in the same family could be so different." The point overlooked is that the children do not grow up in the same family at all. There was no sibling to rival the firstborn, and the "decision" to be a "good child" was made quite unconsciously in response to the perception that "they" (the power figures) seemed to be more pleasant when s/he did as they desired. The second born makes the same observation, but soon discovers that the competition is too strong since the older child is already much more adroit at being "good." Thus, the only course open is to create attention-getting situations in order not to be ignored.[11]

The fact is that although the second-type child appears to be the one in difficulty, the distress of the first-type is just as severe, if not more so. We have seen that, in the biblical pattern, it is the second type rather than the first type who is blessed. The need for forgiveness in the first type is often obscured; yet it is no less real than is the need in the second type. Effective pastoral care and counseling is grounded on an awareness of the fact that both types are hiding, cut off from life-giving relationships, and struggling for meaning.

The positive outcome of forgiveness for both is their increased capacity to respond in a fashion that is appropriate to the realistic situation. The first type comes to the place where s/he can stand against the pressures of life rather than crumble in conformity; the second type comes to the place were s/he can stand with the group in constructive community rather than needing to call attention to him/herself by atypical behavior. In each instance the determining factor is, How can I deal most realistically and constructively with this situation? rather than conforming or rebelling as a means of hiding. It is in that sense that what is done is consistent with and evidence of genuine love of God, others, and self.

There is one final word incident to the implications of the first- and second-type person for pastoral care and counseling. By definition, the minister will tend to fall into one or the other of these characteristic forms of response. In the counseling encounter his/her own pattern of hiding is revealed most sharply at those moments when the relationship taps his/her inner anxieties. Then it is s/he may find her/himself tending to excuse or excoriate, not in terms of the situation of the parishioner, but in response to his/her own needs. Only in appropriate consultation and supervision is it possible to offset this tendency and deal with the parishioner on a basis that makes for growth in openness and creativity.

# III

In the pastoral interviews discussed below, we have opportunity to identify these characteristic first- and second-type responses and evaluate the effectiveness of the minister in each instance. Both of these interviews are from tape recordings, with the data changed sufficiently so that confidentiality is protected.

## A

The minister who presented this first pastoral conversation for consultation noted that she was not entirely satisfied with the way she had dealt with the parishioner. She was aware of the intensity of the inner feelings of Ms. B., and upon reflection realized that she found herself drawn to her to the extent that she had difficulty in staying with the inner anguish. Put in other words, she was caught in the web of protecting and diverting rather than engaging in the kind of realistic encounter that would provide opportunity for the parishioner to deal with her fears.

The parishioner is a woman in her early twenties who has moved to the city following graduation from college. She has an apartment by herself and is employed as a secretary in a law firm. Three weeks earlier she had asked the minister for an appointment "to talk over some things." During their first meeting she expressed general dissatisfaction with her life; "things really have little meaning." The excerpts given below are from the third interview. She has deplored the fact that other people seem to be able to "be themselves" while she cannot. B = Ms. B., and M = Minister.

1. M.   I get the feeling that sometimes you get caught up in the dramatics of the struggle so much that you sort of lose track of things . . .

2. B.   *(Laughs)* I know it . . . and I'm like that all the time, but I shouldn't be that way here . . . you know . . . *(pause)*

3. M.   I get a feeling that you sort of impose something on life . . .

4. B.   Yeah . . . I know . . . and I noticed . . . uh, that . . . I felt you deciphered that out last time . . . you know, when I didn't . . . *(pause, very softly)* no right words . . .

5. M.   You are crying . . .

6. B.   I know . . . *(pause)* I know . . . uh . . . because that is what I do . . . you know I get carried away with making it sound good, and I am not really telling it like it is . . . but I don't know how to sit here and tell my story without *(long pause)* . . . putting on all the unnecessary things because that is how I have been doing it . . .

7. M.   Just feel dragged . . . feeling dragged sometimes when you do that all the time . . .

8. B.   Yeah . . . *(very softly)*.

The parishioner is aware of her hypocrisy and facade of false appearance, and deplores it; at the same time, she feels trapped in it and wonders if she can ever respond in any other fashion. The statement in 4 B is one of both hope and fear: "did you find me out, last time? If so, what will you do?" In 5 M the minister deals with her overt manifestation of emotion, but fails to respond to her uneasiness of whether or not the minister will be "for her" now that she has seen through the facade to some extent. In 6 B she returns to her concern regarding how the minister is feeling about her, and once again 7 M avoids the direct encounter. Perhaps a response here that both defined her true feeling and at the same time Ms. B's uncertainty would have been helpful to her in opening the door. "I'm willing for you to tell me what you wish in any fashion or at any pace you want; even so, you wonder how I am feeling about you, what effect your covering up has on me . . ."

A little later in the conversation Ms. B has said that she supposes she embellishes things since she sees herself as a person who is not really very interesting. The minister responds:

9. M.   You . . . you don't feel you are a person who is very exciting . . . very worthwhile, is that what you are saying? Sounds like you have felt that for years . . .

10. B.   Yeah, I tell you, I think you are right . . . uh . . . for the longest time the criterion for having people like you was just doing . . . going along and—uh, not necessarily crowd following, but people . . . uh, you get a . . .the easiest way out was always the way that it seemed to occur to me and my family to do and it was easier to go along with people . . . it was easier to . . . arguing has no place in my family and in my life. I don't know how to argue, I can't do it. I am inhibited about doing it even when I don't quite agree with you, I'm inclined to say . . .

|        | well, yes . . . and then go about and do it my own way whether I have agreed with you or not . . . |
|--------|-----------------------------------------------------------------------------------------------------|
| 11. M. | When . . . when I say things to you that you may be feeling are not quite right, you go along with it . . . |
| 12. B. | Uh . . . not with you . . . or so far not yet; but usually that is how it is. Somebody says something and they are describing the way I am supposed to feel . . . and I'm not feeling that way, but it just takes so long to explain how I really am feeling . . . they really don't want to hear it . . . so, well, "Yeah, you got it about right." You know, you say, "Yeah . . ." |
| 13. M. | It sounds to me as if you are saying people don't really feel that you are worthwhile. |
| 14. B. | Well . . . |

"If they knew who I am, they wouldn't love me." Here, again, is evidence of the deadly facade that both protects and destroys. The minister finds it difficult to keep the focus of the conversation on what is happening between herself and the parishioner. Her reply in 11 M moves in that direction, but she is turned aside by Ms. B's response in 12 B. It is true that she (Ms. B) indicates she has thus far not caught herself attempting to manipulate the minister; but she follows this with the word noting her fear that this is what will happen. At 13 M the minister turns away from the present encounter to "people," and in so doing, avoids or ignores the crucial relationship between them. Some sort of direct response such as, "I don't know about other people, but I do know that I am very much interested in how it really is with you; yet you're afraid you'll find yourself unable to tell me how you really feel," would have provided an opportunity for her to deal with the reality of her own hiding.

The poignancy of the facade as a means for avoiding rejection is illustrated in an exchange just a few minutes later in the conversation. The parishioner is speaking of her relationship with her parents, and says:

15. B.    . . . I don't know why, . . . in my household full of love and of warmth that a . . . I . . . it seems that maybe my other brothers and sisters . . . all four of us have gotten the feeling that . . . to be accepted by them or by anybody . . . it goes back to dissent . . . dissent means that you likely . . . you know, dissent causes trouble, and if you speak out against it . . . you just stir something up and so why don't you just agree and go along and if you want to do it, just sneak behind their back . . . but, it's . . . I find that—I find myself still trying to . . . uh, trying . . . oh, it's so frustrating. I would like to, uh . . . *(pause)* not that they would stop loving me, but if I would ever just expose myself to them I always thought I would be rejected and I had to be in complete harmony with them in order for them to like me.

16. M.    So there is a fear in you that if you say who you are and what you feel they'll not love you anymore.

17. B.    Yeah . . . except I can't imagine them ever not loving me but, uh . . . for the longest time it was . . . I would say something just to see my father smile at me and say, "Oh, isn't she a clever little girl," or, "Yes, that was

very sweet, Sarah," or you know . . . "My, what a nice, beautiful daughter I have . . ." Saying things that I don't mean but that I know will get a favorable response from my parents and I can't imagine why I lingered in the need to have their response for so long, to have them think that, yes, I was . . . you know . . . the good daughter, and why is that so important?

18. M.   I get a feeling of someone having waked up and looked startled at all the years trying to get approval.

"Maybe if I do what they like, they will love me." The parishioner is conscious of the hypocrisy, the sham, and yet imprisoned by it. "I do not understand my own actions" (Rom. 7:15). But the reason is there, clearly set forth in her anguished words, "if I would ever expose myself to them . . ." "Whoever finds me will slay me" (Gen. 4:14). The minister's response in 18 deals with the retrospective aspect of the statement rather than with the bondage. To focus on the fear, the irrational compulsion, the longing to be loved would have provided a more direct means for reestablishing the broken relationships. For whatever reason, the minister found it necessary to move toward objectivity and solution rather than stay with the pain. In the statement that followed, the parishioner described her feeling about her second-type brother:

19. B.   Yeah . . . *(blows nose)* . . . yeah . . . but approval from your parents . . . you know . . . like your parents *(pause)* the last people you need to worry about . . . not that you

133

don't want to be concerned with them and considerate of them . . . but they are the last ones you have to worry about . . . and it's odd . . . my brother who is sixteen got in bunches of trouble last year and I was really up in the air about it for awhile because it really gave me courage . . . you know . . . here is my brother doing all these things and my parents are worried sick to death about it. I don't want to worry my parents, but at least my brother is doing what my brother wants to do . . . and they, of course, they love him. I knew they would love him . . . I knew they would love me if I did something, but it sort of reinstated it and made me think . . . you know, my brother's doing all these juvenile things gives me courage *(laughs)* to do *(pause)* to do things. *(pause)* You know, I witnessed him doing things that they didn't approve of and I witnessed . . . you know . . . their loving and caring and . . . uh . . .

20. M.    You feel there is a possibility now that you can do some things . . .

21. B.    Yeah . . . yeah.

Here the parishioner is saying that from a conceptual point of view she *knows* that her parents would love her no matter what; but that makes little if any difference in the way she responds to them—or to life. This is another way of saying that "the words are right, but the tune is wrong." Her hesitance belies the conceptual affirmation, and her fear remains. It is unfortunate that in 20 the minister dealt only with the positive side of the ambivalence. For whatever reason she was unable or unwilling to stand with Ms. B. in the agony of "knowing" what is right, but being unable to do it. Something like, "You see a possibility now, but the old uncertainty still clings" at 20 M would have affirmed her in the struggle and avoided the implicit expectation of the minister that this new course now be followed. In the consultation, the minister was painfully aware of the way her genuine longing for Ms. B. to break out of the painful patterns stood in the way of her moving at Ms. B's pace. As it was, she continually moved ahead of her, saying in effect, "Now see, you don't need those old fears any longer." And since the old fears persisted, Ms. B. was pushed back into the facade of not letting them be seen by the minister. "If she sees that they are still there now, she will be disappointed in me!"

One additional factor evident here is that even though the minister is talking with Ms. B. "alone," there are many other persons "in the room." Primarily she is responding to her family of origin, but the patterns developed there carry over into her daily life and, more importantly, in her relationship with the minister. And it is as she can begin to experience forgiveness and affirmation from the minister that she will find herself no longer quite so vulnerable, needing to maintain the facades and defenses. For the minister's part, the consultation provided a perspective that enabled her to meet Ms. B. in a more realistic fashion, not needing to protect her to excuse her but able to encounter her in truth and grace.

## B

The second pastoral interview is with the Green family. They sought help from the minister when their younger son was caught taking drugs at school and was perceived as a behavioral problem by his teachers. The parents, Frank and Betty, had been called to the school to discuss what they intended to do about Jack, the younger son. They agreed to see their minister, who requested that both sons be included in the conference. They demurred at first, noting that Ralph, the elder son, "never gave us a minute's trouble, and we don't see why he should have to be dragged into this." Nevertheless, the minister persisted and they agreed.

In presenting this interview, the minister stated that the family was fairly regular in attendance at worship although he had little contact with them other than that. He had called in the home, but often Frank was away; "He spends a lot of time calling on customers at night," was the way Betty put it. Even prior to this interview, it was evident that Jack was the "scapegoat," the "identified patient,"[12] and his parents felt tremendous pressure to "straighten him out before he got himself or them into real trouble." Betty noted that only two evenings a week would be possible for them since she was taking night courses to complete the degree "I gave up to raise the children." The time was set, and all four persons came to the minister's study at the church. This interview, also, is taken from a tape recording with sufficient alteration to preserve anonymity. F = Frank, B = Betty, J = Jack, M = Minister, R = Ralph.

As they entered the study, the family sat in the following fashion: Ralph sat between Frank and Betty, Jack sat next to Betty, and the minister sat in the circle closer to Jack than to Frank.

1.M. I'm glad we could meet tonight, although I am aware that this is a painful time for all of you.

2. F.      Yes, it is. You know the boys, Ralph and Jack. [M: Uh-huh] Well, I suppose there's no reason to beat around the bush. Jack is the reason we're here. He does nothing but cause us trouble, and now his teachers are breathing down our necks. Just this past week we got called to the school because he was popping pills . . . that's so dumb, but par for him! *(His voice grew louder, and he gripped the arms of the chair.)*

3. M.      I sense your anger with Jack and the pressure of having to come in here to discuss it with me.

4. B.      He's been angry all week. Just this morning he yelled that he was furious about having to come, only sick people come for counseling.

5. M.      And I wonder if being here is not also difficult for you as well.

6. B.      Well, yes . . . yes, it is. I never thought we'd be in this situation. Both these boys are basically good . . . *(she pats Jack's arm)*. It's just that . . . Do you think we can work something out?

At the very outset, the lines of tension and force in the family are clearly evident. Frank is resentful of Jack and the situation, whereas Betty tries to calm the conversation and give some support to Jack. Her question indicates her longing that things can be "fixed" quickly, and the family can get on with its business.

7. M.      I genuinely hope so, Betty, although I'm not sure just what that will mean. And I can sense your urgency in wanting a solution.

| 8.B. | I really do . . . We've tried so hard . . . |
|---|---|
| 9.F. | *(Interrupting)* Now, Betty, you can't blame yourself; you've done all and more than anyone could expect . . . It's just that . . . |
| 10.M. | I heard Betty saying that she was somewhat uncertain, and it seems you have a need to defend her . . . |
| 11.F. | I wasn't defending her! I was just telling it like it is! |
| 12.M. | And it irritates you that I thought it sounded defensive . . . |
| 13.F. | Well, it does . . . We're here to talk about Jack, not about Betty and me! |
| 14.M. | I'm willing for that; so far I've not heard anything from Jack . . . |

The family dynamics here are quite similar to those seen in the family discussed in chapter 2, i.e., the younger child being seen as the "problem." The difference here is not only the intensity of the situation because of the crisis in the school but also the way the minister responds to the persons. We saw in chapter 2 how the minister tended to draw back from any encounter, to avoid dealing with the relationships that emerged in the pastoral call. Here, by way of contrast, the minister meets each person in a fashion that focuses on the relationships openly but without condoning or condemning. "Am I hearing you correctly?" underlies each intervention. It is the "Where are you?" or "There you are" that is involved in any redemptive encounter. In 14 the minister opens the way for Jack to speak, but does not coerce him as would have been the case had he said, "What do you have to say about all this, Jack?" This latter question might have been perceived by Jack as a request for rebuttal, for justification; as it was, the minister stated where he was, and left it at that.

15. J.    Thanks for giving me a chance. I guess we're here because some dumb turkey turned me in. Gee, when you can't even trust your friends . . .

16. F.    Well, you'd better start trusting and going straight *(pointing his finger at Jack)*.

17. M.    As I listen, I notice that it is very difficult for you [Frank] to be patient with Jack.

18. J.    Boy! That's an understatement!

19. F.    *(To minister)* What do you mean by that?

20. M.    Well, it just seemed to me that you found it hard to listen to what Jack had to say . . .

21. F.    Are you taking up for Jack?

22. M.    I don't think so; my hope is to explore with you all the things that are causing so much pain and frustration right now . . . Yet, it seems you hear this as taking sides . . .

23. F.    Well, it sounds like it . . . *(a bit less intensity)*

24. B.    Well, I'm always accused of taking sides. And have been for some time!

25. F.    She does take sides! Never around when I need her but right there when Stupid here does some fool thing!

26. J.    I'm NOT STUPID, you turkey! *(Glares at F.)*

27. M.    Right now my fantasy is that you, Frank and Jack, are like two prize fighters slugging away in the ring while you, Betty, serve as referee trying to separate them; and you, Ralph, are outside the ropes ringing the bell

for them to get back to their corners.

28.R.    Wow! That's us, all right. Only thing is, I beat on the bell, but they don't pay any attention to it!

29.M.    And that's frustrating for you, trying to break up the fight and being ignored!

We said earlier that most ministers will not engage in family counseling. As is evident the minister in this situation has considerable experience in working with families, and at every point strives to meet each person where he or she is while at the same time maintaining an open relationship with all. The responses of Ralph and Jack demonstrate the first- and second-type person, Ralph wanting everything to be smooth and unruffled and Jack needing to act out his frustration by irritating behavior. We can see that Frank, Betty, and Ralph believe that if Jack would behave properly, all would be well. The tragic dimension lies in the fact that Frank's behavior relieves them of the necessity of dealing with their own distortions. It is this factor which lies behind the minister's relating to each of them in terms of their own dynamics rather than siding with them in the attempt to "straighten Jack out." The conformity of Ralph is just as deadly as the rebellion of Jack, and the minister is concerned for both of them as well as for Frank and Betty. It is this understanding that makes possible a wholeness for them all, which includes repentance and reconciliation where each is able to deal with his/her weaknesses as well as his/her strengths. The conversation continues:

30.R.    That's the truth. Mother and I are ignored all of the time; I feel sorry for her since she

|        |                                                                                                                                                                                                                                                                                                                                                            |
| ------ | ---------------------------------------------------------------------------------------------------------------------------------------------------------------------------------------------------------------------------------------------------------------------------------------------------------------------------------------------------------- |
|        | can't get away; as for me, I'm clearing out to go to college . . .                                                                                                                                                                                                                                                                                          |
| 31. J. | You lucky turkey . . .                                                                                                                                                                                                                                                                                                                                      |
| 32. M. | You sound relieved that you can get away, Ralph . . . And I sense you'd like to do the same, Jack . . . Just fed up with the whole outfit . . . *(He nods.)*                                                                                                                                                                                                 |
| 33. B. | Don't worry, Ralph; I'll be OK. We're proud of your acceptance at the University, and I know you'll come out at the head of your class; we never have to worry about you . . . *(Ralph fidgets a bit uncomfortably while Jack breaks a shoelace trying to tie his shoes.)*                                                                                    |
| 34. F. | I'm still back at your fantasy, and I don't like it . . . You've missed the point entirely! We're here to talk about *his* problems, but you've implied that we are all involved . . . You tell us what to do to get him off dope . . . for all we know he may be pushing it!                                                                                 |
| 35. M. | And you resent my not responding the way you thought I would . . .                                                                                                                                                                                                                                                                                          |
| 36. F. | That's for sure!                                                                                                                                                                                                                                                                                                                                            |
| 37. M. | Well, I appreciate your honesty, and hope I can respond in the same fashion. In the short time we've been together I've become aware that there are several struggles in the family, all painful . . .                                                                                                                                                      |
| 38. F. | What's that supposed to mean? Jack caused this whole mess, and it's his doing that makes us worry.                                                                                                                                                                                                                                                          |
| 39. M. | Even though I am aware of Jack's trouble at school it seems to me each one of you is feeling alienated and angry because you are                                                                                                                                                                                                                             |

not heard or appreciated *(Betty fumbles for a tissue and begins to cry).*

40. F.     For heaven's sake, quit that, Betty. She just cries at the drop of a hat, recently. Why don't you wait until there's something to cry about!

The intensity here is practically overwhelming, but it serves to illustrate the kinds of pressures that lie behind first- and second-type responses. Ralph will attempt to avoid involvement by "being good," and thus staying out of the struggle; Jack will attempt to avoid involvement by "being bad," and thus not having to deal with his inner yearning to belong. Frank and Betty are desperate, finding themselves caught in the web, and seeing no way to escape. The minister's interventions are designed to relate to each realistically while at the same time not take sides either for or against. Frank manifests a sense of helplessness, which is threatening to him as Betty cries. In 37 and 39 the minister says, in effect, "I'm for all of you, and long for you to experience the kind of wholeness that comes in relating positively to one another." The conversation continues:

41. M.     Her crying upsets you, Frank; yet, Betty, I can feel a sadness in you, and, it seems, a yearning for Frank's support . . .

42. B.     Oh, yes! Yes! *(Cries)* . . . I want him to hold me, but there's always something between us . . . He's always so busy, customers, trips, I don't know . . .

43. F.     Betty, that's a lie! You *know* I have time for you . . . and I work hard so you can have what you need—clothes . . . *(She cries*

|         |                                                                                                  |
|---------|--------------------------------------------------------------------------------------------------|
|         | *again.)* Now I've said something wrong! I can't do anything right!                               |
| 44. J.  | You TURK!                                                                                          |
| 45. F.  | Don't you ever say that again. I'll . . . I don't like to see her cry . . . I'll get anything you want me to . . . just don't cry . . . |
| 46. M.  | I believe you, Frank . . . It hurts to see Betty cry, and you're torn between your anger at Jack and your wanting her to stop . . . |
| 47. J.  | He deserves it. . . . All the time thinking he can smooth things over by buying us something. . . . We see his money but not much of him . . . |
| 48. R.  | Cool it, Jack, before you cause all of us more grief . . .                                         |
| 49. M.  | Right now I feel the pain in all of you and find myself wondering if this kind of blaming and attacking goes on at home . . . |
| 50. R.  | Right on. . . . There's very little peace in our home. . . . I stay out of the ring because fights tear me up . . . |

The helplessness that we saw in Frank is now clearly evident in them all. The minister may be tempted to "rescue" them with some sort of "there, there, I'm sure we can work all this out." The fact of the matter is that such a glossing over or withdrawing has brought them to this crisis. And the minister knows very well that the crisis provides a priceless opportunity for the patterns of hiding to be set aside, not because they are roughly snatched away, but because there is opportunity for being heard and loved in the presence of the anguish. Little by little, the facades are removed; and the minister does not

chastise them or excuse them; rather he stands with them
as they are. It is important that the minister resist any
subtle tendency to be sympathetic with one or more of
the family members. He might begin to defend Betty as
she cries, or Jack as he is buffeted. Any such move would
hinder the process of reconciliation by blunting the
necessity that each person both be forgiven and forgive.
The conversation continues:

51. B.    Ralph, we don't really fight all that much;
          you're reading, and I'm so busy with my
          classes at school I don't have time to hear
          myself think. . . .

52. F.    Well, you're not the only one that's busy.
          Some of us are trying to earn a decent living,
          and what thanks do I get? A crying wife, a
          son who does nothing but read books, and
          another who is on dope . . .

53. J.    I'm NOT on dope! I tried to tell you that I
          took another kid's Valium because I was so
          upset about something that happened to
          Mike at school, but no one would listen to
          me . . .

54. M.    As I listen to each of you separately and as a
          family I feel deeply the heaviness of your
          isolation and loneliness, and the destructive-
          ness of your resentments for each other. My
          hope is that we can work together to
          experience other ways of relating to each
          other, and be delivered from the hurt and
          anguish that cuts into you all . . .

55. F.    All I want is a little respect rather than so
          much flak!

56. M.    I believe you, Frank; and through all of this I

hear Betty and Ralph and Jack saying much the same thing, longing for respect and appreciation . . .

57. J.  That would be the day! If I was ever appreciated without strings maybe I wouldn't have to take Valium . . .

58. B.  Maybe you're right . . . *(Looks at minister.)* Maybe Jack isn't all to blame. . . . I sure hate to think that we had anything to do with his taking Valium. . . . We really have worked our way into a mess. . . . And now that you mention it, a little respect in our house would be a welcome visitor . . .

59. F.  That's sure the truth. Who is going to start it?

We break off the interview here as the salient aspects of family involvement in first- and second-type response are already quite clear; and, by the same token, the implications for effective ministry are evident in the way this minister demonstrated genuine care for each person in his/her own right and as a part of the whole. The lessening of the tension and the beginning openness to relate in new fashions is not seen as the "solution" of the situation. As was the case with the young businessman in chapter 3, the way toward wholeness is long and there are many dark places to be encountered along the path. The basic factor here is the minister's refusal to "excuse" or "punish," to "condone" or "condemn." By the process of relating in grace and truth the opportunity is opened for each of these persons to find a new life in relationship to themselves, others, and God.

## C

In the first pastoral situation in the chapter we saw the typical response of the first type and some of the opportunities and obstacles encountered by the minister in working with the parishioner. In the family setting just discussed we could see more clearly the interlocking dynamics of family structures that underlie the first- and second-type reactions. In this final, brief situation, we have opportunity to see the second-type and the way the minister attempted to be of help.

The "parishioner" in this instance is a boy of twelve who is attending a summer camp. He is sent to the chaplain after an incident in which he was reported to have threatened a fellow camper with a knife. The chaplain reports that one of the older boys had wrested the knife out of the boy's hand. As he appeared at the chaplain's cabin he seemed shaken; he was half crying and hiding his face. In the verbatim reconstruction C = Chaplain and D = Dick, the boy.

1. C.    Dick, I understand you've gotten into some trouble. Would you tell me what happened?
2. D.    Bill is always teasing me. He threatened to hit me with a shovel the other day.
3. C.    It's not fun to be teased, is it?
4. D.    I was only teasing him. I wasn't going to hurt him. Sometimes Bill and the other boys call me names and make fun of me.
5. C.    It really hurts to be made fun of, doesn't it? Would you like to tell me a little more about what happened between you and Bill?
6. D.    Bill had called me a name, and it made me mad. He was lying on the cot, so I held my knife over his head. I was only teasing.
7. C.    That's kind of a dangerous way to tease, Dick.
8. D.    Yeah, I guess it is. . . . I didn't mean it! (*Sobbing and hiding his face.*) (*I had learned*

*that the patrol leader came in and told Dick to give him the knife. After a few seconds he had lunged at him and taken it.)*

9. C. I would imagine it kind of scared you when Mike came in, is that right?

10. D. Yeah . . . I don't ever want to see that knife again . . .

11. C. It kind of scares you that something like this could happen.

12. D. *(Nods affirmative, still tears in his eyes.)* I don't ever want to see the knife again . . . my new knife . . . I never thought this would happen . . .

13. C. Dick, I know it is very hard to be teased, and awfully tempting to want revenge. I can understand that you were just teasing, but can you see how hard it would be for Bill and Mike to know this? A knife is a very constructive instrument for scouting, but when it is wrongly used, it is a dangerous weapon. *(Dick had quit crying, looked ashamed, and was nodding his head yes to what I was saying.)* Dick, would you like to stay on at camp for the rest of the session?

14. D. *(Looks up with hope.)* Yeah!

15. C. I don't think anything like this will happen again, and I am going to recommend that you stay.

*(Dick stayed; I talked with Bill and Mike. There were no further incidents, although Dick was estranged from the group and wanted to sleep in my cabin. I'm not sure I was much help to him; probably spent too much time solving the immediate problem.)*

The concluding notes of the chaplain deal directly with one of the most crucial factors in working with second-type persons. There is always a tendency to solve the presenting problem, and in so doing neglect the meaning of the problem as the person's way of attracting attention. Ironically, the more time spent on the problem, the more likelihood there is that other asocial behavior will emerge. In this situation, although there were no more incidents, Dick was estranged from the group and unable to be a part of the activities of the camp. We are not told whether he, in fact, did sleep in the chaplain's cabin.

In 3 C, the chaplain seems to stand with the boy, although the "is it?" tends to require agreement. In 5 C he begins well, but the final sentence indicates the chaplain's concern with data, a clear indication that he is moving toward problem-solving rather than attempting to relate to Dick in a fashion that can lead to reconciliation. Then 7 C is judgmental ("Don't you see how wrong you are!"), and the boy's attempt to justify himself shows that he is feeling separated and afraid. Theologically speaking, as long as he is made to defend, there is no possibility of his being forgiven, since forgiveness is experienced only with confession, "Here I am." Unless and until the person knows that s/he is known, any word of grace is irrelevant.

The chaplain momentarily moved toward Dick in 9 C and 11 C, saying, in effect, "There you are; I love you." And in response to this good news we can see a shift in Dick's response at 12 D. Here is the beginning of reconciliation, the opening of the door. Tragically, the chaplain moves back toward moralistic coercion in 13 C, and the possibility for Dick to abandon the asocial behavior is set aside for the time being. The behavior has accomplished its purpose, i.e., gained some attention, but only at the cost of further alienation. The chaplain has "bought into" the ploy, and only in retrospect realizes that his shortsighted goal of solving the problem was attained at the expense of the person.

As we have noted on several occasions, the presenting problem is of importance since it gives access to the person. This does not mean that no solution is needed if one can be found; it does mean that only when the person is kept as the primary focus will the solution have any lasting importance. If, at 13 C, the chaplain had been able to maintain his focus on the parishioner rather than the behavior, he would have opened the possibility for resolving the problem as well as restoring the person. Something like, "I didn't either, and I'm sorry it did; you and I both know how dangerous a knife can be, and it terrifies you to realize how you could allow yourself to be pressed this far. . . ." In this realistic encounter of truth and grace is the good news of restoration and the reestablishing of the broken relationships.

## IV

The ploy of the first- and second-type person, i.e., conformity and rebellion, not only serves as means for hiding but also produces pain and distress. If the ploy did not "work," then it would be discarded; if the ploy did not produce pain, then there would be no possibility for freedom and reconciliation.

It is this tension that is inherent in every pastoral counseling experience. The paradoxical fact that the person both longs for relationships and fears them has been evident in each interview we have examined. In the following chapter we look at the dual struggle more closely as we turn our attention to the theme "death and rebirth."

# Chapter Five
## *Death and Rebirth*

Woven through all the biblical narratives and the case material we have examined thus far is the perplexing and paradoxical aspect of the human situation seen in the fact that the person longs for health and resists it at the same time. Inherent in the resistance is the fear of being found, the terror of dropping the facade, the agony of opening the door, in a word the prospect of death. "Whoever finds me will slay me." However painful and distressing the present situation, at least it is familiar. And so there is a "clinging to evils we now have rather than flying to others we know not of." Moreover, there is a destructive self-deception that accompanies such ploys and strategies. "This behavior is not really 'me,' and I can forego it at any time; but it does 'work,' it does provide some relief, it does protect me from the unbearable prospect of risking relationships on an open and honest basis." At a deeper level, it protects against a true being of the self. "I am unable to admit to myself who I really am." So goes the inner dynamic, although not very often is it a part of conscious awareness, and seldom if ever the basis for overt decision. Thus, the first-type person does not enjoy maintaining the facades of conformity, but does so since they do produce a bit of approval. The fact that they take away far more than they provide seems irrelevant at the time. In like fashion, the second-type person does not enjoy the constant rebuff and difficult consequences of his/her behavior, but continues to act in the asocial fashion because there are temporary benefits. The resistance to health lies in the simple yet unthinkable fact that only as the protective devices are given up can newness of being emerge. But to do so is to risk death, a reality inherent in the biblical concept of "rebirth." In essence, the person actually "dies" to the old and destructive patterns, and is "born" into the new.[1]

# I

The figure of "death" and "rebirth" helps in our understanding of the struggle of the person in the contradictory longing for health and wholeness and resisting it. This biblical theme provides still another facet for a deeper understanding of the work of the minister as counselor.

"Do you want to be healed?" (John 5:6). On first reading, this question of Jesus seems incredible on its face. The man has been ill for thirty-eight years, has daily been brought to the pool of Bethesda in hope of some miracle, and has never recovered. The fact is, however, that the question makes very good sense. Whatever may have been possible many years ago, it is fairly evident now that healing would present many problems for the man. He has apparently had someone to feed him and bring him to the pool. If he becomes well, he will have to fend for himself. Moreover, no sooner has he begun to carry his pallet away than he runs into trouble with the religious authorities. We may assume that he had encountered no such opposition before. As the story ends, he seems to be in greater jeopardy. Jesus' parting words to him are ominous, indeed: "See, you are well! Sin no more, that nothing worse befall you" (John 5:14). Implied in this admonition is the notion that if the man slips back into his old patterns, his last condition could be worse than the first.[2]

The theme begins, however, not in the New Testament but in the Eden narrative. The hiding of the man and his wife, the twisted, devious stories designed to shift attention from the self, the facade of the clothing attest to the resistance that is everywhere evident in the human struggle. How hard is it for Adam to realize that the searching question "Where are you?" is the voice of reconciliation. How hard in the Gospels to know that "God sent the Son into the world, not to condemn the world, but that the world might be saved through him" (John 3:17).

Although the theme of resistance to change runs throughout the pages of the Old and New Testaments, one of the clearest manifestations of it occurs in the Jacob saga, and it is to that we turn our attention for an understanding of the meaning of the resistance and the fashion in which it may be overcome. In examining the story, five segments stand out. These are: (1) the experiences at home; (2) the dream at Bethel; (3) the experiences with Laban; and (4) the struggle at Peniel; (5) the reunion with Esau.[3]

The pattern of Jacob's life-style is graphically described in the birth experience where he takes hold of the heel of Esau, his older brother. He is a trickster, a supplanter, one who will live by his wits and his prowess, his ability to manipulate and stay just ahead of the consequences. Here, again, is the strange reversal wherein the "elder shall serve the younger" (Gen. 25:23). The cryptic comment in 25:27-28 indicates the extent to which the behavior of the two brothers is a reflection of the tensions between the mother and father, as well as a result of the satisfactions that the behavior won which assured its continuance.

The two incidents that sketch the rebel ploy of Jacob are his tricking Esau of his birthright (26:29-34), and his tricking Isaac of the "first-son" blessing (27:1-40). In the latter, he is aided and abetted by his mother who also works out the flight to Haran not only as a means for saving his life (27:41-45) but also in order to assure that he will find more acceptable wives than had Esau (27:46). Although not part of the Yahwist text, it is significant that in this latter venture he is encouraged by Isaac, a move that motivates Esau, the first type, to try desperately to do that which will please his father (Gen. 28:1-9, esp. v. 9). Thus the die is cast. Jacob, the supplanter, has managed to "win," and escape the consequences of his trickery. The very fact that he has eluded the necessity to deal with his own perfidy now becomes a factor in his resistance to openness and wholeness since he must bear the burden of the treachery and the fear of consequences.[4]

The second segment of the saga is the experience at Bethel. Here, cut off from the roots of the familiar surroundings, Jacob lies down to sleep. The well-known dream of the ladder set up on earth reaching to heaven with the angels ascending and descending and the Lord God standing above it is an affirmation of grace. "Behold, I am with you," the word that comes at the point of fear, is spoken just when the future is unknown and uncertain. Nevertheless, Jacob is ambivalent about being found. Does God come to punish? "Then Jacob awoke from his sleep and said, 'Surely the Lord is in this place; and I did not know it.' And he was afraid, and said, 'How awesome is this place! This is none other than the house of God, and this is the gate of heaven' " (Gen. 28:16-17). In characteristic fashion, Jacob sets about to turn the events to his own gain. His bargain with God, a bargain to which he will appeal in time to come, is evidence that he has in no sense abandoned his ploy as a means for survival and success. He leaves Bethel as he came, still the trickster and manipulator.

The focus of the story moves to Haran and the events surrounding Jacob's dealing with Laban, his marriages to Leah and Rachel, and his trickery in turning the tables on his father-in-law so as to assure gaining the upper hand as he leaves. But the success of his ploy does not come easily. In Laban, he has encountered one as devious as himself. Having worked seven years in order to marry Rachel, he discovers that he is married to Leah, the older sister. Thus Laban requires of him yet another seven years before the marriage to Rachel is completed (Gen. 29:1-30). It is as Jacob is preparing to leave that the battle of wits reaches its climax. Laban thinks to thwart the agreed upon wages by treachery, but Jacob outmaneuvers him and departs with the best of the flocks, leaving Laban with "the feebler" (Gen. 30:25-43). "So Jacob arose, and set his sons and his wives on camels; and he drove away all his cattle, all his livestock which he had gained, the cattle in his possession. . . . And Jacob outwitted Laban" (Gen. 31:17-18, 20). Once again, the ploy has succeeded, and the resistance to change increased.

As we follow the story to the fourth phase, it becomes clear that the consequences of the past are now catching up with Jacob. He is returning to the land of his fathers, and there he must face Esau. At the same time, he is pursued by a hostile Laban, who overtakes him in the hill country of Gilead (Gen. 31:25). There the encounter is played out to a stalemate. Jacob protests that he has more than earned all the wealth, while Laban stoutly maintains, "The daughters are my daughters, the

children are my children, the flocks are my flocks, and all
that you see is mine" (Gen. 31:43). When it becomes clear
that there will be no change, they erect a pillar of stones to
mark a dividing line between them. Laban called the
pillar "Mizpah, for he said, 'The Lord watch between you
and me, when we are absent one from the other.' . . . 'See
this heap and the pillar which I have set between you and
me. This heap is a witness, and the pillar is a witness, that
I will not pass over this heap to you, and you will not pass
over this heap and this pillar to me, for harm' " (Gen.
31:48, 51-52). Thus, as Jacob continues his journey
toward Esau, there is no way he can retreat.[5]

Jacob now faces an even more terrifying encounter. He
sends messengers to Esau to work out some sort of a
solution. But the messengers return with the ominous
word that Esau is "coming to meet you and four hundred
men with him." Understandably, "Jacob was greatly
afraid" (Gen. 32:1-7). Here, again, we discover the fear of
Adam, the wail of Cain. Jacob is caught between the
pincers of Laban behind him and Esau before him. His
final strategy is the division of his company in the hope
that, when Esau attacks, one or the other will escape.
Then he appeals to God, reminding him of the promise at
Bethel, crosses the ford of the Jabbok, and "was left
alone" (Gen. 32:7-24).

It is here that "a man wrestled with him until the
breaking of the day" (Gen. 32:24). In this mysterious
struggle with the night figure, the terrible strength of
Jacob's style of life is revealed. Only toward the breaking
of the day when it seems as though the "man" will not
prevail, he touches the hollow of Jacob's thigh so that
"Jacob's thigh was put out of joint as he wrestled with
him" (Gen. 32:25). In that moment Jacob loses—and
wins. No longer is he to be Jacob, the supplanter; now he

is Israel, he who strives with God. As he receives the blessing, he calls the name of the place "Peniel, saying, 'For I have seen God face to face, and yet my life is preserved' " (Gen. 32:30). Through the terrible encounter he experiences the incredible reality that the consequence of his being found is not death but life.

The completely unexpected epilogue to the story is the reconciliation with Esau. Still fearful of what Esau may do, Jacob moves toward his brother, proffering gifts by means of which he hopes to gain his favor. It is difficult for the old pattern to die completely. "But Esau ran to meet him, and embraced him, and fell on his neck and kissed him, and they wept" (Gen. 33:4). The parallel between this and the action of the father in receiving the prodigal is unmistakable. "But while he was yet at a distance, his father saw him and had compassion, and ran and embraced him and kissed him" (Luke 15:20). Jacob's efforts to bribe are turned aside by Esau with the words, "I have enough, my brother; keep what you have for yourself." Jacob cannot believe what is happening and implores Esau to receive the present, not as a bribe, but as a gift born of gratitude, "for truly to see your face is like seeing the face of God, with such favor have you received me." It is in this spirit that Esau accepts the gift (Gen. 33:1-11).

In this closing drama, all the factors of reconciliation are acted out. We are given no hint to explain how Esau, hostile and vengeful when Jacob left, now appears as the true "elder brother" who forgives and restores. Nevertheless, the figure of Esau in Genesis 33 and the figure of the father in Luke 15 demonstrate the nature of forgiveness, which resists the ploy of the person forgiven, accepts him without condition, and affirms his personhood in the new relationship, which is based no longer on strategy but on genuine and creative love. Esau's acceptance of Jacob is not because of the gift, just as the father's acceptance of the prodigal is not based on his offer to work as a hired servant. The acceptance is born of grace, and in response the person is enabled to drop the deadly ploys and facades, to die, and in dying discover life as a "new being." The acceptance of the gift as a gift is the mark of the true "elder brother," and demonstrates the corporate nature of the reconciliation, the reestablishing of the broken relationships which is marked by communion, a giving and receiving.

## II

The implications of the theme of "death and rebirth" for pastoral counseling are crucial. Before turning to several illustrations, we explore three primary dimensions that emerge from the biblical data.

In the first place, there is the recognition of what has been called the "secondary gains" of personal problems. However distressing the situation experienced by the person, it is far from unambiguously negative. The variation on the old adage "Hell hath no fury like a woman scorned—unless it be a neurotic deprived of his symptom" expresses well this basic factor in the tendency of the person both to desire deliverance and yet maintain the distress. In recent years, it has become commonplace to note that alcohol is not the alcoholic's problem, rather it is his/her way of attempting to solve the problem. Deep within are feelings of guilt, of remorse, of self-hatred, of failure, of bitterness, of hopelessness; and, as many alcoholics have asserted, for a few hours there is oblivion in which none of these agonizing feelings can torment an already battered self-concept. No matter at this moment the awareness that after the oblivion the pain returns many fold; at least for now it is gone, the alcohol has "worked." The same destructive dynamic is evident whatever the presenting behavior. So it is that the parishioner who participates in a counseling experience with the minister "needs" the painful behavior at some level or other and is terrified at the prospect of giving it up. This is the sense in which Jacob finds that his trickery continually results in difficult consequences, but struggles at Jabbok to maintain it since it is the only way of life he knows, and since it has, in fact, brought tangible gain.

The second aspect that informs the work of the minister as counselor is the awareness that the person in the interview brings to the experience the exact ploys and strategies that are being described in one form or other as occurring in the narrative of his life. Although we have identified this factor from time to time in previous situations, its underscoring here takes on new meaning in our discussion of death and rebirth. It is not unusual for the minister to fall into the trap of assuming that in the counseling conversation both s/he and the parishioner are somehow separated from the ordinary patterns of behavior, that by some mysterious process they are delivered from their "life-styles" during this hour and can contemplate, discuss, analyze, and resolve those ploys which in day-to-day existence bring distress. Only the realization that whatever happens "out there" also happens "in here" will prevent a losing of the battle before it is ever begun. It is precisely the dealing with the relationship being experienced between the two that any hope of renewal is possible. This relationship is the "stuff" of healing, and only as transformation occurs here can it occur at all.

This focus on the relationship in the counseling interview is not to imply that the resources of life come only through the pastor. We have already noted the sense in which nurture is corporate, that the parishioner draws on the totality of life for continued sustenance. It does mean, however, that the counseling interview is a microcosm of life, it is part and parcel of that which is continually happening. The essential difference between counseling and care, as we have seen, is the concentration of the relationship, the artificiality of the setting of time limits and occasions for meeting, the focus on the here and now throughout. It is this intensive encounter which provides the possibility for the person once again to draw on the life-giving resources of daily living which have been disrupted through the negative consequences of the characteristic ploy. The counselor, to be effective, recognizes the importance of responding not in the fashion of those who for whatever reason have been influenced by the ploy, but in a manner that resists and, indeed, goes contrary to the ploy. The ensuing struggle is, in fact, the parishioner's resistance to death; but as it is maintained by the minister, it opens the way to new life where the destructive ploy is no longer needed.

This brings us, in the third place, to the necessity for the minister to resist the ploy at every point, however intense the struggle. Inevitably, the person perceives the resistance of the ploy as a rejection of the self, since the ploy is experienced as the only means for survival. To be sure, there are often verbal protestations that the ploy is to be abandoned. Such folk behavior as New Year's resolutions illustrates the sense in which all persons from time to time determine to change, to turn over a new leaf, to respond to pressure or threat in a different fashion. The tragic fact, of course, is that it simply does not happen. At best, the decision lasts only a few hours or days, at which time the old pattern takes over again. At worst, the old pattern is replaced by one more deadly still as vividly depicted in the parable describing the return of the demon with seven more deadly than himself. So it is that in the counseling relationship, the person has an opportunity to experience the meaning of genuine relationships apart from which life is impossible and thus can now drop the facades and ploys that represented a protective hiding from any direct and open encounter.

In general terms, it is ordinarily true that the ploy of the person in distress takes one of two forms. Either there is the attempt to coerce the counselor into accepting the person's definition of reality and move on that acceptance; or there is the attempt to have the counselor assume responsibility for the parishioner's life, to make decisions, give advice, and remove any necessity for personal participation in the ambiguities and consequences of living. In common parlance, this is usually referred to as the parishioner's "wanting to push the minister around," or "wanting the minister to push him/her around." It is only as the minister is able to resist both of these pressures that there is hope for recovery. Put in other words, only as the person meets a person who responds openly and honestly is it possible for him/her to become a person.

The consequence of this encounter is painful, not only for the parishioner but also for the minister. As was true of Jacob at Jabbok, it is an agonizing struggle and at times there are wounds. Without being overly dramatic, it is possible to say that whenever the pastor and the parishioner engage in counseling, one will "die." Not "death" in any literal sense, although occasionally that does occur; rather, death in that the person's ploys will be withstood in the direct encounter and ultimately dropped, or the person will "kill" the minister by some such means as negative comments to others about his/her ability or effectiveness.

The nature of the encounter is, therefore, marked by constant attention on the part of the minister to define his/her own identity as the way s/he sees reality. Complimenting the focus on "there you are," which we have stressed as essential for reconciliation, the emphasis here is on the minister's saying "here am I." In commenting on definition while discussing previous conversations, we have called attention to its necessity when the person asks, when it seems that the person's view of reality does not correspond to that of the minister and when it seems that the person has incorrect assumptions regarding the minister's attitude, intention, or belief. Such definition is not in any sense intended for the purpose of imposing a structure or position on the parishioner. Rather, it is intended to provide the possibility for a realistic encounter between the two individuals. Thus, the definition is always made in the context of a return to the parishioner's frame of reference. The meaning of the definition and return is bound up in the words, "Here I am, there you are, and I love you." The actual demonstration of this factor is seen in the conversations set forth in the next section.

# III

In the three pastoral situations that follow, the struggle of death and life is seen in the pressure placed on the minister by the parishioner in varying forms. All three are verbatim reconstructions of actual conversations.

A

The parishioner in the first conversation is a student in second-year graduate school who called the university chaplain for an appointment. Although she had met him on one or two occasions, she indicated that she really knew very little about him. He arrived at the agreed hour, and was met at the office door by the chaplain. In the conversation, C = Chaplain, J = Jim.

1.C.    Good afternoon, Jim. Will you come in?

2.J.    Thank you. *(He enters, hesitates a minute, and takes the chair by the desk indicated by the chaplain.)* I do appreciate your seeing me. I . . . I guess I need some help . . .

3.C.    I'm glad you've come, although I'm sorry for the occasion that brings you. Things haven't been going well, I take it.

4.J.    No . . . No, they really haven't. *(Pause.)* I'm really not too sure what to say . . . Uh . . . Where would you like me to begin?

5.C.    Well, I'll be guided by your judgment. . . . Now that you're here, you're sort of uncertain what to do . . .

In the chapter on "initiative and freedom" we discussed the notion of contract, giving particular attention to those occasions when the minister goes to the parishioner. The establishing of the contract is much more overt when the parishioner comes to the minister. Here, in 2 J, the student says, "I need some help." In 3 C, the minister responds, indicating that she is willing to accept his request and work with him toward a possible resolution of the difficulty. As the conversation proceeds, the nature of the contract is revised from time to time as different expectations are brought out which the minister accepts or rejects depending on her own perception of herself, the parishioner, and the relationship. Just how this happens is illustrated in 4 J, where the parishioner introduces the first refining of the contract, i.e., "your help is needed to show me where to start." Although such a statement is not unusual, in most instances the parishioner moves rather quickly to recounting some situation or feeling which is troublesome. An understanding of contract as involving not simply a "problem out there" but the total dimension of the relationship enables the minister to recognize that the request for help in "starting" is no less a dimension of the process than any other factor that may emerge. In this conversation, that request turns out to be of paramount importance.

The notion of when the pastoral counseling conversation "begins" has often been overlooked. We saw in chapter 2 that the introductory remarks may be one of the most crucial dimensions of the interview. It is here that the basic assumptions are manifest, and it is here that the minister may find her/himself trapped before s/he realizes that s/he has already taken a course of action that will turn out less than helpful. I can recall countless verbatim reconstructions presented by students and ministers that include at the beginning some such phrase as "after pleasantries, the parishioner said. . . ." Only gradually do many ministers realize that the pleasantries may carry the key to the relationship.

Nowhere is this more evident than in the seemingly simple question, "Where shall I begin?" The hidden assumption behind the question is that until certain data are being discussed the counseling conversation has not begun. Such an assumption grows out of problem-oriented counseling as contrasted with person-oriented counseling. So it is that all too many ministers find in themselves a kind of "ah, at last" feeling when the parishioner begins to talk about this or that distress. The same perspective causes these ministers to deplore the fact that "it was hard to keep the parishioner on the subject." But when the relationship between the two is "the subject," such a complaint does not occur. An understanding of this factor is crucial in any effective pastoral counseling.

Very often, verbatim conversations reveal that the minister responds to the query of 4 J with some such reply as: "Well, wherever you wish. Maybe you'd like to tell me just what it was that prompted you to call for the appointment." Close inspection reveals that the two sentences are self-contradictory. Moreover, as soon as the minister has designated the course of the conversation, the present relationship has been abandoned for the time being. A variation on the above response is, "Well, just begin where you were when you called." Of course the person can never "begin" there since s/he is no longer there. S/he can talk about this "history," but already it is being filtered through the experiences of the now. The chaplain, in the conversation recorded above, was aware of the fact that the "beginning" was already long since past. Thus, she moved to the student's uncertainty as the primary factor in their present relationship.

6.J.     Yes, that's right. You see, I've never done this before, and I want to make the most of the time we have. . . .

7.C.     So do I. Are you saying that you'd be more comfortable if I would suggest an area for you to discuss . . . ?

8. J.    Yeah . . . Actually, I'm perfectly willing to tell you anything at all, but, as I said, I don't want to waste your time by talking about things that are unimportant.

9. C.    I see. It would be hard for me to think of anything you might say as unimportant, but, even so, you'd feel better to have my suggestion as to a topic . . .

10. J.    Well, yes. . . . You've been doing this a long time, and you know what things are profitable and what things aren't.

11. C.    As a matter of fact, I don't really; I'm not against suggesting an area, it's just that I really wouldn't have the vaguest notion of what it would be . . .

12. J.    *(Interrupting.)* Oh, now, don't give me that! I didn't come here for you to play games with me!

13. C.    It's certainly not a "game" with me . . . but it kind of irks you to think I'm not being honest with you . . .

14. J.    Yes it does! I told you I will be willing to talk about anything at all, but I don't appreciate you not being willing to meet me halfway!

15. C.    I certainly intend to meet you halfway, although it doesn't seem like that to you; and it irritates you that . . .

16. J.    *(Interrupting)* It certainly does! I'm not sure I should have come!

As the chaplain fails to meet the student's expectations, he finds himself becoming angry. He resents what seems to him as a refusal to a legitimate request and begins to question whether he will continue. This is a crucial point, and there is no way to predict the outcome. He comes, as do all persons, with definite expectations of how the counselor will function. When these expectations are not met, the tack is to redouble the characteristic ploys in order to produce compliance; and, correspondingly, a resistance toward relinquishing the ploys that have been useful to a degree but that constantly bring difficulty. When the minister does not perform in the desired fashion, he may in fact break off the relationship. This consequence of human freedom, as we saw in chapter 2, is an ever-present threat to the minister. How difficult it is to allow "rich young rulers" to walk away! And here the minister may be sorely tempted to acquiesce just a bit in order to prevent the parishioner's withdrawing. It is the person's way of saying, "If you *really* care for me, you'll do what I want," a ploy that is deadly for both if the minister does not resist.

17.C.  I'm sorry to disappoint you. You're wondering whether or not this is really worthwhile . . .

18.J.  Well, yes . . . I do wonder . . . but now that I'm here, we'd just as well go on. Maybe I should tell you something about my childhood . . .

19.C.  If you wish . . . Is it that this seems to you a likely area?

20.J.  I guess so. . . . I've understood that childhood is very important, and thought maybe if I told you about that you could help me see how things get so tangled up. . . . But, goodness, there is so much . . . it'd take forever to tell it all. Maybe if you'd ask me a question or two we could get into it . . .

21.C.    Well, again, let me say I'm not essentially
          unwilling to do that; it's just that I honestly
          haven't any idea what kind of question
          would be helpful . . .

22.J.     Aw, now . . . I know that isn't so. . . . And
          besides, just a couple of questions would get
          me going . . . you know . . .

23.C.    Seems so reasonable to you . . . hard to
          understand that I really am telling you the
          truth . . .

24.J.     Yeah, it is. . . . You're just bound to know
          what is the best place to start, what will help
          me . . . just a little . . .

The attitude of the parishioner changes from irritation
and anger to plaintive supplication. The chaplain
continues to affirm her own identity, while at the same
time attempting to identify with him in his struggle with
her. It is not an easy task, and in presenting the material
for evaluation she noted that on more than one occasion
she found herself hard-pressed to "stay with him," as she
put it. Although the above verbatim conversation can be
read in a comparatively short while, the actual conversation went on in this vein for over thirty minutes. The
parishioner resorted to one means after another in order
to get the chaplain to designate a place to start.

As I have used this particular conversation in pastoral
conferences as well as seminary classes through the years,
it has often evoked considerable resistance on the part of
the participants. Many have felt that it would be
impossible for such a conversation to be sustained for over
thirty minutes, that the person would long since have
broken off or told the chaplain *something*, however
irrelevant it might appear. To this criticism I can only

reply that in this particular situation the conversation did happen as recorded; at the same time, it is evident that this is extreme and that ordinarily the pastor does not encounter a circumstance at such a level of struggle over the issue of "beginning." Even though it is uncommon, however, the conversation serves to illustrate the extent to which the parishioner attempts to manipulate the minister into following a predetermined course of action.

At a deeper level, many experienced counselors have disagreed with the procedure of the minister on the ground that it tended to increase the person's anxiety to such a degree that any future relationship might be impossible. Moreover, these persons have said the issue is not of that much importance. A few questions to start the ball rolling could not possibly have any long-range negative effects. The point, ultimately, is nondebatable. In this particular situation, the pastor *did* respond as indicated, and the person *did* continue in the relationship toward positive growth. Whether in another situation the person would have broken off, and whether a slight compromise might have affected the maintenance of the relationship, is speculative. In the story of Jesus and the rich young ruler it is significant that no such compromise was suggested as he went away. Whether the parallel can be so closely drawn may be a matter of opinion. It has been my experience through the years that the gain in such a compromise is not worth the cost, although the possibility for recovering lost ground following less than helpful counseling certainly does remain. If that were not so, most ministers would give up the task altogether. But the fact that this is so is scant justification for ineffective procedure.

In the interview itself, the time came when the student said,

25. J.     Well, it's clear to me you aren't going to be of help. So I guess I'll just have to start somewhere . . .

At this point in seminar discussions, I have often asked if anyone would care to speculate on what words followed this statement. It may be that the reader will, before going on, wish to hazard a guess on the "presenting problem" as identified by the student when finally he decided to "start."

25. J.     (*Continuing.*) It's just . . . well, . . . from the time I was a little boy, I was never allowed to make a decision. . . . My mother decided everything, even after I got older. She picked out my clothes, she chose my friends, she told me what college I would attend, she thought my coming here for graduate work was just the thing to do. It's been terrible, and . . . and . . . now, well, I'm just not capable of making up my mind about *anything*. . . . I've wanted to talk with you for the longest time, but just couldn't . . . and Friday one of my friends actually dialed the number for me when I called. . . . You can't imagine what a hell it is. . . . Here I'm grown . . . and I'm paralyzed over having to cope as an adult. . . .

It would be difficult to find a more striking illustration of the fact that the parishioner's behavior in the counseling interview is the same as that which "outside" is causing the distress. There is no way we can know what might have been the outcome if the chaplain had taken

over the decision for him as to where to begin. It is certain
that she would have found herself in the very trap which
had proved his undoing through the years. As it was, her
continued refusal to be swayed by his manipulative ploy
and her continued manifestation of concern for him as a
person in the midst of his struggle provided the context
wherein he could take a tentative step toward opening the
door. As would be expected, the struggle was not over
after 25 J; but the positive course evidenced by 25 J had
been established. As a footnote, I had an opportunity to
see Jim in a professional conference several years later,
and was gratified to note the effectiveness of his
functioning not only in his chosen field, but also as a
person.

### B

The second pastoral conversation is quite different, but
illustrates the resistance to wholeness. In his prefatory
statement the minister indicates that Mr. Howard (Bob)
had been hospitalized for alcoholism several years before,
but had continued drinking intermittently since his
release. He is married, and he and his wife (Elizabeth)
have two married children, both living some distance
away. Unlike many alcoholics, Bob had remained fairly
regular in his church activities although it was common
knowledge that when he was absent he was usually
drinking. He was self-employed, managing a small
business with some ten or twelve employees. More
recently he had suffered some financial reverses (some
related to his drinking), and Elizabeth had started
working part time to help out. On the Sunday of the visit
recorded below, neither Bob nor Elizabeth were at
church; word was that Elizabeth was visiting her sister in
a nearby town and Bob was probably drinking. The

minister concluded his remarks by saying that he had called in the home on various occasions, but did not relate the substance of any prior conversation. Following morning worship, the minister phoned the Howard residence, but there was no answer. He decided to go by later that afternoon. B = Bob, E = Elizabeth, M = Minister.

> *(I [the minister] knocked on the door, and after a short wait Bob answered. He was unshaven and looked thin, even haggard.)*

1. B.     Uh . . . uh . . . well, hello, Steve. . . . Won't you come in? . . . Excuse my appearance, I haven't shaved today. . . .

2. M.     Thanks. . . . I missed seeing you and Elizabeth at church this morning, and wanted to come by to see how things are . . .

3. B.     Ya . . . Well, I've been sort of under the weather and tried to take it easy. . . . Elizabeth is visiting Judy this weekend . . .

4. M.     So you're here by yourself . . . *(By this time we were seated in the den.)*

5. B.     Yeah. . . . To tell you the truth, I don't feel so hot right now. . . . It's been like this for a while, just feel punk most of the time. . . . Don't know what's the matter with me . . .

6. M.     I'm not real sure why you feel so bad, either; but it seems to me you've been drinking pretty much lately and that may be the problem. . . . Really, that's why I'm here. . . . If I can be of help, I'd like to . . .

In discussing the conversation later, the minister noted that he was not able to give a forthright definition at 2 M, although that was the proper place. Only at 6 M did he reveal his true purpose in calling. His reticence clearly stemmed from his uncertainty as to how he could broach the subject in a constructive fashion; at a deeper level, he was aware of the fact that such an encounter would open the way for a direct attack on him and he was ambivalent about engaging in the struggle. Despite his hesitation, he was on sound ground when finally he stated his position. His definition includes his perception of the situation and his concern for Bob; he makes no categorical claim, such as: "See here, you are a drunk! What are you going to do about it?" As far as it goes, this is constructive. However, he might have been a bit more diligent to affirm Bob's freedom by concluding with some such word as, "I may be clear off base, and if so I need to hear that from you, and I'll apologize for speaking out of turn."

Ordinarily when the minister takes the initiative in this kind of painful encounter, s/he can expect one of three responses. The parishioner may engage in denial with some such word as: "Well, Reverend, I appreciate your concern; but there's really no problem. I may have had a bit too much now and then, but everything's OK. Are things going well with you and your family?" When this type of brush-off is encountered, the minister does not press the point. Rather s/he speaks of family (or whatever) and shortly leaves, still voicing concern for the parishioner, and the hope that they can keep in touch.

The second typical response is anger and attack. "See here, who do you think you are barging in here like this. If you haven't got enough to do minding your own business, then maybe you'd better take a second look!" Here, also, the minister takes such a word quite seriously. S/he knows that there is probably a great deal of unresolved hostility in the person, and if s/he can enable it to be expressed in a context that will not condemn, then the parishioner has the possibility of dealing with life at a less volatile level. Something like, "Bob, I certainly have more than I can say grace over in my own life; yet I do care about you; even so, you resent my being here, and would like it just fine if I'd leave." Having said that, the minister waits for the next response from the parishioner, and on the basis of what is said remains or leaves according to where the parishioner defines him/herself.

Finally, the person may, in effect, collapse. "Thank God you're here. I'm at the end of my rope, desperate. . . . I've wanted to call you, but am too embarrassed and ashamed. . . . Do you think you can really help?"

The fact is that none of the three possible responses completely opens or closes the door. The first two seem to be denials, but may shift as the minister is sensitive to the subsequent statements. The third may seem to be an invitation, but may represent a person's relinquishing his/her participant responsibility by saying, in effect, "You take over!" No matter which is paramount, it is certain that the other two will also be present to some extent or other. The conversation continues:

7.B.   Well, I suppose I've been hitting it pretty hard lately . . . no secret about that. . . . At least not in this neighborhood!

8.M.   Sort of resent everybody knowing your business, is that it?

9.B.   I sure do! Why can't people mind their own business! Like I've told you before, I don't do anybody any harm! A few drinks never hurt anyone; and I need a couple when things go bad at the store just to calm my nerves. . . .

10. M.   Well, I can hear that; you get so up-tight you just can't stand it any longer. . . . Thing that worries me is that it seems you're doing *yourself* a lot of harm even if no one else . . . and I imagine the business is bound to suffer when that happens. . . . Yet, my guess is you know that, and feel the need for a drink anyhow . . .

Here the struggle is joined. Bob sets forth the inner pain that he resolves through alcohol; and the minister communicates his understanding of the resentment and the stress, but is not drawn into a sympathetic stance that would excuse the behavior. At 10 he stands against the ploy, but with Bob. The conversation continues on this vein, and shortly thereafter, the following exchange occurs:

11. B.   You've no idea what it is like to try to run a business in this day and age; regulations choking you to death, employees demanding more money; merchandise going sky-high, pricing you out of the market; it's hell, Reverend, if you'll excuse the expression . . .

12. M.   So the time comes when you're at the end of your rope . . .

13. B.   That's right! That's it exactly! I don't know which way to turn. . . . And now Elizabeth has gone to Judy's, and . . .

14. M.   Sounds like you are desperate . . .

15. B.   I guess that's right. . . . But what can I do? I

went to the hospital a few years ago but they
didn't help me. . . . They said it was an
illness; but if it is, then they should have
cured me . . .

16. M.    If I remember right, you did get sober and
looked a lot better. . . . I don't remember
your following the program they suggested,
or going to A. A. My impression was that you
decided you didn't really need all that; I may
have missed it, but I gathered you were
saying it was the doctor's fault that you didn't
get any better, and now you hesitate to go
back . . .

17. B.    I suppose so. . . . Guess I really didn't do
what they said. . . . If I go back now, will
you go with me . . . just to help me check in?

18. M.    Yes . . . but I want us to call Elizabeth so she
can be in on this, too . . .

19. B.    Aw, I don't know, Steve. . . . She's pretty
well washed her hands of me . . .

20. M.    And that's painful. . . . Even so, I want us to
get in touch with her, and let her say where
she is . . .

This verbatim reconstruction is condensed; even so,
the movement of the conversation is important. The
minister is constantly aware of Bob's resistance to facing
up to his own involvement, his own responsibility; at the
same time, he is conscious of the pain that in this situation
is one of the best allies Bob has, even though it is not so
perceived. The intention of the minister is to stand with
him, not instead of him or against him. It is a thin line, as
is seen in 16. Here he sets forth his perception of the
situation without condemning or condoning. The fact that

the parishioner heard this as an affirmation both of him and of reality, i.e., grace and truth, is evident in his plea of 17. The minister knows that there is a long road ahead; but he is also aware that they are now moving in another direction. Bob's admission of helplessness attests to the agony of death that leads to rebirth. At this moment, he is in a kind of never-never land; the road to recovery is possible but not inevitable.

So it is that the minister moves toward bringing Bob's wife into the situation. He is aware of the fact that alcoholism, as is true of any other personal distress, is not an individual problem. Elizabeth is certainly enmeshed in Bob's problem drinking. Just how this is so is not yet clear; in any event, her presence is crucial, both in the hospitalization and in what follows. It is tragic as well as ironic that often the spouse of an alcoholic will marry another alcoholic following the death or desertion of the first. Such behavior, however irrational on the surface, bespeaks the fact that in time s/he comes to "need" an alcoholic, however painful the relationship may in fact be. As long as the alcoholic is there, the spouse's negative attitudes and behaviors are excused both by the person and by his/her friends and relatives. "What you put up with, dear; I don't see how you do as well as you do!" Such a word is deadly; however true the painful circumstance, there is never solely the negativity of the alcoholic in the relationship. Thus, for Elizabeth's sake as well as Bob's, the minister properly recognizes the needs of both.

As it turned out, Bob called Elizabeth, and she came to the hospital that evening, having driven back from her sister's. The minister met them both there and arranged for both of them to come in to his study following Bob's release. In the brief interchange given below, a part of the first joint session is set forth.

21. E.    He's doing a lot better, I'm glad to say. These past few months have been terrible, and I'd like to put them behind us forever. . . . But . . . *(trails off)*

22. M.    I hope so in the sense of not having to go through them again. . . . Right now you're hopeful, but not sure . . .

23. E.    Yes, I am. . . . I still don't know whether I can count on him. . . . Tell the truth, I don't even know why I am here. . . . Really, all he needs to do is stop and everything would be OK . . .

24. M.    Well, my impression is that both of you have a lot of hurt, and I'd like us to work on things together; even so, you have real reservations . . .

25. B.    Actually, Steve, it *is* all my fault; but believe me, this time it's different . . .

26. E.    He always says that, but it doesn't mean anything. . . .

27. M.    You tell *me* that. . . . Wonder how it would sound if you said it to Bob . . .

28. E.    He already knows it . . . just doesn't do anything about it . . .

29. M.    And you resent that very much, so much so it's hard to talk to him right now. . . .

30. B.    Goodness knows she *has* told me enough!

31. M.    Sounds like you're pretty well up to here in the telling. . . .

32. B.    That's right! I feel badly enough as it is without her on my back . . .

Even though brief, this segment of the pastoral interview clearly demonstrates the basic tension and resentment between Bob and Elizabeth. On her part, she can't see that any of the "problem" is her responsibility, as is evident in 23. Bob abjectly takes all the blame in 25, but his true feeling comes out in 30 and 32. The fact is that in this kind of encounter with the minister present to provide support for both of them, there is tremendous possibility for growth. The minister's effectiveness rests upon his constant awareness that there is no such thing as a "guilty" person and an "innocent" person in any relationship. However much one may seem to be at fault, as is the case here, both contribute in one sense or other. The necessity for death and rebirth is as real for Elizabeth as it is for Bob. If they can experience genuine forgiveness and reconciliation, then the destructive attitudes and behaviors will no longer need to be employed. In that event, it is not that one "wins" and the other "loses." As was true of Jacob at Jabbok, both will lose, and in the process both will win. The following is an excerpt from an interview about ten weeks later.

33. B.　I was thinking as we were driving down here that I really look forward to our times together; sure different than when we started . . .

34. M.　I do, too. . . . It's not been easy for you, or for Elizabeth, and it's nice to breathe a little better . . .

35. E.　Yeah. . . . Sometimes I wonder if I'm the same person. . . . I'd gotten where I couldn't depend on Bob for anything. . . . And, actually, I was running the show . . . writing the checks, paying the bills, seeing about household matters. . . . I guess I really took over so that he was pretty much left out. . . . But I was afraid . . .

36. M.   Sort of, "If I don't do it, it won't get done . . ."

37. E.   That's right! . . . And that's not the way to be. . . . If we are going to be in this together, we've got to give and take more . . .

38. B.   I agree; but I didn't leave you much room. . . . I was off on cloud nine, somewhere. . . . You didn't have much choice . . .

39. M.   Are you saying that you're uncomfortable when Elizabeth says something about the way she let herself get boxed in?

40. B.   Yeah . . . Yeah, I guess so . . .

41. E.   The fact is that I did that, and now I don't like it. . . . I don't want it to be that way anymore, no matter what happens to you . . .

42. M.   That says to me you want to take responsibility for yourself, not get pushed into a role you don't like . . .

43. B.   That makes a lot of sense, but it scares me, too. How do I know I'll do OK?

44. M.   You sure don't want to let her down, again . . .

45. B.   Or myself, either . . .

46. E.   That cuts both ways . . . I don't want to let *you* down, or me . . .

The difference between this conversation and the first following Bob's release from the hospital is dramatic. The recriminations, the blaming, the defensive strategies are practically absent; both Bob and Elizabeth are intent on assuming their proper responsibility for themselves as well as for each other and their relationship. There is risk here in that the minister may reach the unwarranted conclusion that everything is now all right. A closer look reveals that both Bob and Elizabeth are hesitant to depend on the other. In drawing back from demanding, they are unsure of what is appropriate to expect in the give and take of marriage.

The concept of "death and rebirth" is quite evident here; but it would be incorrect to think of it as a kind of all-or-nothing experience. Rather, in biblical perspective, it is a process with gains and losses. The positive dimension is that increasingly the gains outweigh the losses as the husband and wife find it possible to bear each other's burdens, and to allow the other to bear his/her own load (Gal. 6:2, 5).

## C

We turn briefly now to still another facet of the resistance encountered in death and rebirth as seen illustrated in the matter of time limitation for the interview, itself. We noted earlier that the counseling relationship is not essentially different from any other relationship in kind, but is basically different in degree. One atypical dimension is the designation of a time for beginning and ending the interview. It is essential that this limitation be clearly set beforehand so that both pastor and parishioner(s) are aware of it. If the parishioner calls for an appointment, the simple response is: "Yes, I am free from three to four on Tuesday. Is that possible for you?" If the parishioner comes to the church without an appointment, asking if there is time to "talk over some things," the response is the same as that above if the minister has a full calendar; if, on the other hand, s/he has time just then, the termination is set by some such word as: "Yes, I'm free just now until 4:15. Will you sit down?" The person may demur that s/he needs only about fifteen minutes, and if that is actually the case, then the conversation is concluded earlier. However, in the event that the parishioner does, in fact, have much more to say, then there is no awkwardness at the conclusion.

The matter of designating sixty minutes for the appointment is purely arbitrary, based simply on the realistic division of the day into such segments. If the conversation goes on beyond an hour, the law of diminishing returns tends to set in. Covertly, there is communicated the unrealistic expectation that "if we talk about this long enough, we'll solve every phase of it." The truth is that much of the growth occurs between the interview times as the person begins to relate to the real world in a more open fashion. The end of the hour provides an opportunity for the parishioner to move out of the intensive focus of the relationship, and for the contract to be reviewed, i.e., "Shall we continue or not? And if so, on what basis?"

Usually, the minister finds it most beneficial at the end of the first session to offer to see the parishioner one week later if there is still more to be discussed. Some such word as, "I'm free this time next week if you'd like to return," is adequate. There is value in the regularity of weekly conversations, the rhythm of moving into and out of the intense experience. Much of the value is lost if the sessions are scheduled haphazardly. During the interim the parishioner does what might be called "homework," not in the sense of anything that is assigned, but in the sense of thinking back over what was said and contemplating what will be said on the next occasion. The regularity of appointments provides a structure for this kind of inner process which is absolutely essential for any lasting growth.

If the parishioner fails to appear for the appointment, or continually asks for a change in day or hour, this is ordinarily an indication of the unwillingness to get well and becomes the focus of the conversational encounter. It may well be that the person is not, in fact, ready to deal constructively with the critical issues, in which case the minister respects his/her freedom. By the same token, the minister refuses to "play" at counseling by acquiescing to haphazard meetings. The time comes when s/he says, clearly: "Either we set a schedule and stay with it, or stop altogether. I am not able to work in this hit-or-miss fashion. I want to work together with you if you wish, but have begun to wonder whether this is really what you want." Such a forthright definition is designed to clarify the contract. The minister sets his/her own limits and leaves the parishioner free to move in either direction.

Alongside the matter of regularity of meeting is the adherence to the time schedule of the interview hour itself. If the parishioner continually arrives late, then this factor becomes the focus of the conversation. Some such statement as, "I notice that you are always about ten minutes late, and am puzzled about this." This self-definition is quite different from the ordinary question, "Why are you always late?" or "What does it mean to you that you are always late?" The latter two place the person on the defensive, call upon him/her to justify him/herself, and in so doing remove him/her from the personal encounter to conversation about the encounter. The former, by dealing with the feelings of the pastor, keeps the focus on the relationship and provides for the kind of personal encounter that opens the way for growth.

In the conversation excerpt that follows, the parishio-

ner (P) is resisting the termination of the interview with
the minister (M) at the appointed time. This is the twelfth
session, and in several previous hours the matter of going
beyond the limit has been discussed, but not as pointedly
as on this occasion. At about eight minutes before the
agreed-upon termination point, the parishioner says:

1. P.    That damn clock! It's almost at the end of the
hour, and I'm not through . . .
2. M.    You resent having to be bound by this fixed
time . . .
3. P.    You're damn right! What makes you think
that the only time I need you is between
three and four o'clock?
4. M.    I really never thought that, although I
honestly don't believe that if we stayed here
for fifteen minutes or even longer things
would be much different. Even so, it riles
you that I stay with the clock.
5. P.    Yeah. Seems to me you are much more
interested in your silly schedules than in me.
6. M.    That's not really what I intend, but it's hard
for you to see it any different . . .
7. P.    All right, go into your song and dance about
having somebody coming at four o'clock, at
which time you just turn me off . . .
8. M.    Sounds to me like you're saying you resent
my being interested in the person coming in
at four. That you want to be special, sort of
"teacher's pet."
9. P.    Maybe so. . . . Damn it! It's four! All right,
I'll leave!
10. M.    Still angry . . . I'll see you next week, same
time . . . if you wish . . .

The overt manipulation attempted here is not always so clearly evident in the behavior of the parishioner. On some occasions, the ploy is to launch into an involved narrative just prior to the end of the hour in a much more subtle effort to stay beyond the agreed upon time. Still another fashion of such strategy is to begin a sort of "self-debate" as to whether or not to return next week. Whatever the form, the minister may be sure that insofar as s/he succumbs to the ploy, just so far is s/he prolonging the recovery of the parishioner. The parallel of Jacob's wrestling with the night figure, where the "breaking of the day" was the termination, is instructive here. There is a blessing, but there is also no continuation.

In the interview excerpt above, the irritation and resentment of the parishioner become the focus that makes the relationship open and honest. The minister does not argue, does not chide, does not punish; at the same time, she does not capitulate. At every point she defines herself and her own identity, and accepts the resistance of the person as the realistic manifestation of the struggle both to maintain the patterns and to drop them. In this "here I am, there you are, and I love you" encounter, the person is able to experience the possibility of genuine freedom from the shackles so long endured.

# IV

"Do you really want to get well?" The answer is always ambiguous; however overt the desire for freedom, there is an inner fear of facing the responsibilities occasioned by wholeness. It is only as the minister is genuinely aware of this ambiguity that s/he is able to stand against the ploys that seem so essential to the person but that result in such destructive consequences.

The struggle that ensues is always difficult and at times severe. At some point or moment, the minister faces the decision whether or not s/he can run the risk involved in the struggle. If the decision, whether overt or covert, is no, then s/he will capitulate by diverting the conversation to externals, by giving advice or engaging in moral exhortation, by facile reassurances or pious platitudes. Whenever the minister discovers any of these procedures appearing in his/her counseling sessions, s/he can be certain that s/he has given up the encounter that might lead to life. This does not mean it cannot be resumed another day or even in the same session. It does mean that for the time being, s/he has ceased to walk with the person "through the valley of the shadow."

On the other hand, if the decision is yes, then the minister can be certain that the risks to him/herself are high. We noted, in a not overly dramatic way, that in any true pastoral counseling one or the other of the persons will "die." It is to an exploration of this factor that we turn as we consider the biblical theme, "risk and redemption."

# Chapter Six
## Risk and Redemption

As we come to the consideration of the final theme to be explored for its implications in the counseling work of the minister, we are aware that its dimensions have been a part of the discussion all along. Here, as everywhere, each theme involves all the others and is inherent in them. Thus, we have experienced the risk incurred by the minister in standing against the ploys of the parishioner, in struggling with the pain of encounter, in taking the initiative to find the person who is fearfully hiding behind the deadly facades of hypocrisy.

In one sense, everything has been said, even though in suggestive form. In another sense, it is essential to focus finally on the experience of the minister in order to gain a complete picture of the pastoral counseling function of reconciliation. The question is, what happens to the pastor in the experience? As we investigate the answer, the relevant factors emerge from a consideration of the biblical material that illuminates the risk of participating in the redemptive process.

## I

As before, the thrust of the theme is set in the beginning. The stark tragedy of the Yahwist story in Genesis 2 and 3 closes with the man and his wife now outside the garden. No longer is there the openness of relationship that brings life. Rather there is fear and hiding, and the world becomes not only a place of beauty, but also a place of terror. No longer is there the earth yielding its abundance for the nurture of wo/man. Rather the ground now brings forth "thorns and thistles" (Gen. 3:18), and there is enmity between wo/man and the creatures (Gen. 3:15). Bread shall be wrested from the earth in the sweat of the face (Gen. 3:19), and the experience of procreation will be marked by pain and suffering (Gen. 3:16). How far this seems from the eschatological world of Micah 4:3, 4: "and they shall beat their swords into plow shares, and their spears into pruning hooks; nation shall not lift up sword against nation, neither shall they learn war any more; but they shall sit every man under his vine and under his fig tree, and none shall make them afraid." (See also Isa. 17:2; Ezek. 34:28; Zech. 3:15). "None shall make them afraid." It is this winsome and elusive prospect that is the essence of the redemptive experience as we saw in chapter 3 and elsewhere.

The prospect will not be accomplished easily. The man and his wife cannot return to the garden; the reconciliation can be accomplished only outside the walls, as it were, since that is where they are. And, as we noted in chapter 2, it is this search that is the initiating factor in the reconciliation. Just as it is hard for Adam and Eve to allow themselves to be found, so, also it is difficult to engage in the search. The very defense mechanisms that perpetuate the hiding ultimately are directed toward the destruction of the seeker. The word of Jesus to the scribes and Pharisees is paradigmatic: "Woe to you, scribes and Pharisees, hypocrites! for you build the tombs of the prophets and adorn the monuments of the righteous, saying, 'if we had lived in the days of our fathers, we would not have taken part with them in shedding the blood of the prophets.' Thus you witness against yourselves, that you are the sons of those who murdered the prophets. Fill up, then, the measure of your fathers. You serpents, you brood of vipers, how are you to escape being sentenced to hell? Therefore I send you prophets and wise men and scribes, some whom you will kill and crucify, and some you will scourge in your synagogues and persecute from town to town, that upon you may come all the righteous blood shed on earth, from the blood of innocent Abel to the blood of Zechariah the son of Barachiah, whom you murdered between the sanctuary and the altar" (Matt. 23:29-35). As we read these words, vivid scenes from the Old Testament flash across our minds such as Jeremiah in the stocks or the mire of the pit (Jer. 20:2 and 38:4-6). Listening, we can hear the lament of Elijah after the contest on Mt. Carmel, "I, even I only, am left; and they seek my life, to take it away" (I Kings 19:10).

In the New Testament, the theme is supremely manifested in the crucifixion of Jesus, who was put to death "outside the walls" ("the place where Jesus was crucified was near the city"—John 19:20; cf. also Matt. 27; Mark 15; Luke 23) as symbol that forever epitomizes the vulnerability of the person who seeks for another to reestablish the broken relationship. The full meaning of the experience is summed up in the words of Hebrews 13:12, 13: "So Jesus also suffered outside the gate in order to consecrate the people through his own blood. Therefore, let us go forth to him outside the camp, bearing abuse for him."[1]

The risk in redemption, although epitomized in the symbol of the cross and death, is not confined to this extreme eventuation. At every point, the theme of leaving the security suggested by the "walls" is evident in both the Old and New Testaments. The call of the prophets picks up the strain as illustrated in the words of Isaiah 6:11,12: "Then I said, 'How long, O Lord?' And he said: 'Until cities lie waste without inhabitant, and houses without men and the land is utterly desolate, and the Lord removes men far away, and the forsaken places are many in the midst of the land.'" The instructions to Elijah after his anguished cry that he only was left and his life was in jeopardy were, "Go, return on your way to the wilderness of Damascus" (I Kings 19:15). In like fashion, the commission to Ezekiel could hardly be more pointed: "Son of man, I send you to the people of Israel, to a nation of rebels, who have rebelled against me; they and their fathers have transgressed against me to this very day. The people also are impudent and stubborn: I send you to them; and you shall say to them, 'Thus says the Lord God. . . . And you shall speak my words to them, whether they hear or refuse to hear; for they are a rebellious house" (Ezek. 2:3, 4, 7).

In the New Testament, the words of Jesus to the disciples provide the most consistent elaboration of the theme of risk in redemption. In Matthew 10 as he is sending out the Twelve, their defenselessness is summed up in the words, "Take no gold, nor silver, nor copper in your purses, no bag for your journey, nor two tunics, nor sandals, nor a staff" (vv. 9, 10). This seeming lack of resources stands in stark juxtaposition to what will be encountered on the mission: "Beware of men; for they will deliver you up to councils, and flog you in their synagogues, and you will be dragged before governors and kings for my name's sake, to bear testimony before them and the Gentiles" (Matt. 10:17, 18). Perhaps the most compelling description of the risk is contained in the *via crucis* passages of Mark 8:31; 9:31; and 10:33, 34. Here, Jesus speaks plainly of the cross that awaits him when he arrives at Jerusalem, an announcement that fills the disciples with dismay and despair. So great is their anxiety in the prospect that it is for a while doubtful whether they will be able to accompany him on the way. Simon Peter rebukes him, only to be rebuked in turn. Thomas' words in John 11:6 voice in poignant fashion the disciples' awareness of the implications of Jesus' words: "Let us also go, that we may die with him."

The working out of the risk is the hallmark of the New Testament church. Always "outside the walls," the disciples are whipped, stoned, imprisoned, and put to death. The word of the Lord to Ananias, who is reluctant to go to Saul and minister to him, recognizes the reality of Ananias' hesitation to run the risk of dealing with one who has persecuted the church, and also specifies the risk to Saul, who, as Paul, would bring the good news to every corner of his ancient world. "Go, for he is a chosen instrument of mine to carry my name before the Gentiles and kings and sons of Israel; for I will show him how much he must suffer for the sake of my name" (Acts 9:15, 16). It was so. In retrospect, as Paul looks over the experiences of the years, he writes to the church in Corinth describing his "labor," his "imprisonments," his "beatings," and his being often "near death." Continuing, he says: "Five times I have received at the hands of the Jews the forty lashes less one. Three times I have been beaten with rods; once I was stoned. Three times I have been shipwrecked; a night and a day I have been adrift at sea; on frequent journeys, in danger from the Gentiles, danger in the city, danger in the wilderness, danger at sea, danger from false brethren; in toil and hardship, through many a sleepless night, in hunger and thirst, often without food, in cold and exposure" (II Cor. 11:23-27). At every point, the search for Adam is fraught with danger; as the shepherd leaves the ninety and nine and searches for the sheep that is lost, just so the relinquishing of safety inside the walls is the mark of the redemptive experience. It is a costly enterprise to bring the good news to Adam, "There you are; I love you; you are forgiven."

That there is risk in the act of redemption there can be no doubt; yet it would be completely misleading to conclude that those who engage in the ministry of reconciliation are thereby without resources. On the contrary, at every turn there is the strong assurance of the strength and power to accomplish the task in the face of every vicissitude. The point then is not that the risks are nonexistent; rather in the presence of the risks there is that which makes it possible to meet the situation and fulfill the mission of restoration.

To Jeremiah, so beset before and behind with opposition and persecution, comes the word, " 'Be not afraid of them, for I am with you to deliver you,' says the Lord. Then the Lord put forth his hand and touched my mouth; and the Lord said to me, 'Behold I have put my words in your mouth. See, I have set you this day over nations and over kingdoms, to pluck up and to break down, to destroy and to overthrow, to build and to plant' " (Jer. 1:8-10). In like manner, at the time of Elijah's deepest despair, the Lord provided food and drink, and the assurance that there were seven thousand in Israel whose knees had not bowed to Baal or worshiped at his shrine (I Kings 19:5-8, 18). So, also, Isaiah experienced the reality of forgiveness and healing (Isa. 6:7) and the sure confidence that God was working out his purpose in the very presence of the vicissitudes (Isa. 6:13).

The same pattern obtains in the New Testament. As Jesus sends out the Twelve, the fact of their overt vulnerability is countered by the words, "So have no fear of them; for nothing is covered that will not be revealed, or hidden that will not be known. What I tell you in the dark, utter in the light; and what you hear whispered, proclaim upon the housetops. And do not fear those who kill the body but cannot kill the soul; rather fear him who can destroy both soul and body in hell. Are not two sparrows sold for a penny? And not one of them will fall to the ground without your Father's will. . . . Fear not, therefore, you are of much more value than many sparrows" (Matt. 10:26-29, 31). The concluding word to the disciples at the end of Jesus' ministry contains the promise "I am with you always" (Matt. 28:20); and Paul discovered the reality of this assurance in the words, "My grace is sufficient for you, for my power is made perfect in weakness" (II Cor. 12:9). It is in this sense that he writes, "I have learned, in whatever state I am to be content. I know how to be abased, and I know how to abound; in any and all circumstances I have learned the secret of facing plenty and hunger, abundance and want. I can do all things in him who strengthens me" (Phil. 4:11-13).

In summary, to move "outside the walls" is essential in the process of redemption since that is the place where persons are to be found. Such a forsaking of the security inevitably leads to tremendous risks for the one who undertakes it, risks that run the gamut from misunderstanding and rejection to persecution and death. Nevertheless, at every point there is the resource to sustain the one who engages in such a ministry.

## II

As we turn to the implications of the theme "risk and redemption" for pastoral care and counseling, three factors emerge as of primary importance to the minister. We consider each of these in turn before moving to illustrations in actual pastoral experiences.

The first is the realistic fact that pastoral counseling is not a pleasant or glamorous procedure. The myth dies hard that working with people in trouble has about it a kind of special exhilaration and excitement that yields only positive satisfactions for the helper. Somehow there persists the notion that in counseling, the essential dimension is characterized by the type of activity reported by the centurian who said, "I say to one, 'Go,' and he goes, and to another, 'Come,' and he comes, and . . . 'Do this,' and he does it" (Matt. 8:9). The idea is that the counselor is some sort of omniscient "fixer" who is able to search out the proper remedy and apply it so that people are delivered from their distress. Now it is certain that there are genuine satisfactions in participating in the growth process of another person; but this fact does not set aside the painful, frustrating, vexing dimensions of being involved in the life struggle of one who wishes to be relieved of difficulty but resists the very healing which makes the deliverance possible.

I think back across the years to students who have come into a course on pastoral counseling with the unstated assumption that now they will learn the esoteric strategies and procedures that will equip them to dispense wise advice and counsel; and that as they do this, the recipient will "rise up and call them blessed!" There is often painful disillusion in the discovery that such fantasies find no roots in fact. Unfortunately, there are those who somehow manage to hold on to the myth and move out into the ministry with the mistaken notion that once they say the right word of advice, the person will be whole. Such an attitude leads to a growing insensitivity to the inner struggles of parishioners and a reduced capacity to bear the burdens of those whose lives have become to some extent unmanageable.

It is this misunderstanding that makes an experience in a clinical setting under supervision such as that provided by clinical pastoral education programs so invaluable for theological students and clergy. In such a circumstance, the minister is able to gain an increased understanding of the depths of human struggle and to experience at a significant level the meaning of personal bondage. In retrospect, I know that my greatest teachers in my early ministry were men and women caught in the bondage of alcohol addiction. I was fortunate to become associated with persons in Alcoholics Anonymous in the early 1940s, and through the years these people have enabled me to realize the frustration as well as the fulfillment in the human struggle. In doing "Twelfth Step Work" I soon discovered that it was not possible to maintain long the idea of glamor in pastoral counseling while smelling the stench of a dingy flophouse or sitting with a lad on the iron cot of the county jail. These lessons learned in the pain of disappointment through failure as well as rejoicing in success were reinforced in subsequent experiences on the wards of federal and state hospitals for the emotionally disturbed. It is fairly easy to write these words in the peaceful atmosphere of my study; but the experiences were far from peaceful, often frightening and painful, and they are burned into my memory so that I can relive them with a vividness even after the passage of the years.

Perhaps the most disturbing and perplexing aspect of

the nonglamorous dimension of pastoral care and counseling occurs when the person or persons do not perceive that there is any need of help within themselves. Differences of opinion, resentment over various emphases of the gospel, bitterness occasioned by seeming unfair or treacherous actions of others, all these and more are occasions for healing. Yet who is the minister who has not been dismayed or repulsed by attacks on him/herself by irate parishioners for participating in causes that seemed right and needful, including action of the church or support of persons whose lives were caught in the tangled web of evil?

In such circumstances, it is often difficult, and some would say impossible, to move from a defensive or offensive position to one motivated by pastoral concern for the person doing the attacking. It is one thing to listen to Jesus' prayer from the cross for his tormentors or Stephen's petition for those whose stones would shortly take his life. It is something else again to feel the fierce pain of opposition and still maintain an awareness of the inner needs of the person whose anger or opposition is the cause of the pain.

It is here that the minister asks two basic questions, questions that are essential for effective pastoral care. The first is, What truth is there in what this parishioner is saying; what can I learn from this encounter that I did not know or had overlooked? In the press of debate, it is often difficult to allow oneself to be instructed by the position of the protagonist. This is particularly true when the attack is personal. The minister who can reassess his/her action and attitude in the presence of personal confrontation is in a position to "bear the other's burdens." The second question is just as essential, What is happening in this person that makes the attack so vehement and vitriolic? The importance of this question lies in the fact that in the heat of argument, persons often are motivated by hurt, disappointment, and distress quite apart from the issue at hand. A man whose wife is unfaithful, a woman who has been discriminated against because of her sex, a young person who is feeling left out of activities in school or social life tend to lash out with far more emotional charge than the issue warrants.

It is in this context that the theme "risk and redemption" provides a crucial dimension for a comprehensive understanding of pastoral care. In the search for Adam there is danger, heartache, pain, and death. There is also success; but it comes only through suffering, and it may not come at all.

The second implication of this theme for pastoral counseling is the necessity for the minister to be aware of the erosion that takes place within him/her as s/he works with people in trouble. There is a meaningful passage in the New Testament that deals directly with this factor. As Jesus is surrounded by a great crowd, a woman who had suffered from hemorrhage for twelve years touched his garment. She was healed, but there were consequences. The text notes that Jesus perceived "in himself that power had gone forth from him" (Mark 5:30). There is no indication just what it was that happened in Jesus that made the perception clear, but the implications are unmistakable. Any minister who engages in effective pastoral counseling runs the continual risk of the depletion of the self. Such a statement may sound overly dramatic, and it is not so intended. Usually, the erosion is quite gradual, and only later is its devastation apparent if it is not checked. There are several characteristics of the erosion that are useful in assessing its presence.

Perhaps the most pervasive is the inability on the part of the minister to set limits. This often takes the form of difficulty in saying no to various requests, and stems from the desire to be approved by doing that which is acceptable. Inevitably such procedure leads to conflict and frustration, but as the personal strength of the minister is eroded, the urge to please at whatever cost becomes more pronounced. Ministers tend to rationalize such "sacrificial" service on the ground that theirs is a self-giving profession. The fact is that apart from some sort of realistic awareness of limits, there is little "self" to give. It is instructive that ever and again in the ministry of Jesus, he withdrew from those who were demanding his time and attention in order to engage in personal renewal.

The inability to set limits is particularly destructive in pastoral counseling situations. In the former chapter we discussed some of the implications of demands by the parishioner that the allotted time be extended. In addition to this type of demand is the sometimes subtle request that the minister undertake something for which s/he is not qualified. In considering the implications of referral there are two tendencies that often beset the clergy. The first is to refer too quickly, to refuse to participate in personal struggle that clearly is demanding of time and emotional resources. On the other hand, there is the devastating tendency to refrain from referral on the ground that the "gospel" is adequate to meet any situation. Such an attitude is scarcely an affirmation of the power of faith in the healing of the human situation; rather, it is usually a manifestation of pride on the part of the minister who finds it difficult to recognize personal limitations and see him/herself as a part of a wider resource in the alleviation of human misery.[2]

Another dimension of the erosion of the self is seen in the developing of a self-styled martyr feeling. Precisely because a genuine devotion to those things which make for life does in fact produce resistance and distress, it is an easy shift to conclude that the presence of difficulty in personal relationships is evidence of dedication to duty. Such a shift, however, is deadly. The story of the church is strewn with the wreckage of clergy who were unwilling to examine the nature of their own distress in order to determine whether it had arisen because of their faithfulness or their failure. Again, a passage in the New Testament is instructive here. In the sayings of Jesus recorded in Matthew 5, 6, and 7 is the word, "Blessed are you when men revile you and persecute you and utter all kinds of evil against you falsely on my account" (Matt. 5:11). The key word is "falsely," and it is crucial that it be taken seriously by every minister who experiences resistance and hostility. This underscores the need to raise the basic questions: Does this rejection arise because of my own ineptness or lack of concern, or is it a manifestation of the hurt and distress in the person? Unless and until these questions can be asked and answered honestly, the chances of ministry are greatly reduced. I recall with sadness a minister who continually alienated persons because of his own insensitivity to human struggle and suffering. Tragically enough, he always identified the negative reaction of his parishioners and fellow clergy as evidence of his own pure devotion to duty and was never able to examine the possibility that the fault was his, not that of those around him.

Perhaps the most subtle and deadly erosion of the self occurs in what might be called being caught up on the pathology of the other person. The more serious the distress of the parishioner, the more subtle and powerful the ploys to maintain the patterns of behavior that are at one and the same time destructive but perceived as necessary. It is no easy task to avoid the manipulations that are continually a part of such a relationship, manipulations that are not to be condemned but certainly not to be followed. Suggested above in the necessity to set limits, this aspect of the erosion of the self involves a special kind of limit-setting in terms of resistance to the loss of one's own identity. The most prevalent factor inherent in this aspect of the erosion of the self is emotional involvement with the parishioner. We have come a long way from the time when the ideal stance for the person attempting to help another was a strict objective attitude. Whatever else is true about the restoration of broken relationships, it is certain that personal involvement is essential. At every point in our discussion thus far we have been aware of the sense in which the minister feels with the person. There are times when laughter is most appropriate, and other times when tears are evidence of inner pain aroused by the suffering and struggle of another. And precisely because this is so, the risk of loss of identity is greatly increased.

What happens is that the needs of the minister begin to take precedence over the needs of the parishioner. Persons in great distress seem to be highly sensitive to the weaknesses of other people and, as a consequence of this sensitivity, seem to be able to play upon those weaknesses with deadly skill and determination. The erosion process is gradual; but when the point is reached when the minister *needs* the parishioner, then the situation is critical. This does not mean that the minister does not yearn for the person, does not long for the kind of relationship that is creative and lively, does not grieve when the person resists the opportunity to be whole. It does mean that the minister is at every point able to withstand the rejection, to allow the person freedom to walk away, to resist the temptation to maintain a destructive relationship by compromising his/her own integrity. This factor, which has been so much a part of all that has gone before in the discussing of the biblical themes, is underscored here because of its basic importance in any healing relationship. The image of Jesus weeping over the city is paradigmatic. "O Jerusalem, Jerusalem, killing the prophets and stoning those who are sent to you! How often would I have gathered your children together as a hen gathers her brood under her wings, and you would not! Behold, your house is forsaken and desolate" (Matt. 23:37, 38). Here is the epitome of yearning, grief, and pain in rejection but at the same time the refusal to compromise, to yield integrity for the sake of a destructive approval.

The third implication of the theme "risk and redemption" for pastoral counseling, growing directly out of the preceding factor, involves the absolute necessity for every minister to establish some sort of consultative relationship as a means both for assessing the nature of his/her work and as a means for continual self-renewal. It is only in some such situation which includes qualitative evaluation of pastoral experiences that it is possible for any minister to maintain personal integrity and identity. The kind of realistic feedback by someone competent to deal with process and substance of pastoral counseling is essential for any sort of effective ministry.

This notion seems so obvious as scarcely to need exploring. But the sad fact is that too many ministers tend to function in isolation and seldom if ever subject their work to the scrutiny of those who are qualified to evaluate strengths and weaknesses. This point came home to me with telling force when the seminary where I teach instituted a program of continuing education leading to the doctor of ministry degree. Persons who had graduated and served in the parish were able to return to the campus for additional work, which included not only course offerings but also "Competency Reviews." These latter were designed to provide opportunity for the aspirants for the degree to demonstrate their ability to function in a competent fashion in the tasks ordinarily associated with ministry, i.e., biblical interpretation, homiletics, pastoral care, teaching, and the like. Again and again we discovered to our sorrow and to the pain of the person participating that for many years these ministers had literally not had anyone tell them the truth about what they were doing. To be sure, they had experienced their share of criticism, but ordinarily this had been sloughed off as being only a manifestation of the sickness of some church member. In like fashion, they had learned to tune in to the approving remarks of those persons who, with the best of intentions, said only the kinds of things that were pleasant to hear. When, in the course of the reviews, attention was called to this or that area where performance was not adequate, the students responded with shock, hostility, and disbelief. During these experiences, I became aware as never before of the necessity for every minister to have a support system, a group of persons who were willing and able to examine constructively and creatively the various dimensions of pastoral performance.

Nowhere is such examination more crucial than in pastoral counseling. Only in some such procedure is it possible for the minister to maintain that kind of perspective which keeps him/her from becoming swept away by the tremendous demands of persons in distress. It is, of course, painful to have one's work scrutinized by those who are willing to identify the weak places and to call attention to overlooked assumptions. At the same time, such consultation is certain to prevent much greater pain and dismay, which will surely come as a consequence of any and all efforts to function in professional isolation.

The form of such a support system will vary from person to person and from situation to situation. The most likely fashion is a group of peers in ministry who meet with regularity to discuss at a professional level what is happening in their ministry. The substance of the discussion may vary, but at every point it is focused on person and function. Each minister may present, in turn, a verbatim reconstruction of a pastoral counseling conversation or, if available, a tape recording of such a conversation. As the material is discussed, attention is given to what is happening to the *minister* rather than to the parishioner. To be sure, the factors of the pastoral situation are not ignored, but if the consultation is to be of maximum benefit, the minister is the focus and all else is contextual. Such questions as, "Are you saying here what you really intend to say?" and "Do you intend that this attitude be communicated?" and "What does it mean to you to press the person in these ways?" and "Is it possible to deal with the reason why you began to reassure the person here and give advice?" and "Is it possible that you have begun to respond to the subtle pressures and manipulations of the person in these and these ways?" help to concentrate on the minister's personal involvement and performance and serve to keep the perspective in proper focus. The presentations do not need to be confined to pastoral counseling, of course. Sermons, administrative situations, teaching procedures, conduct of worship, and the like are all fit subjects for professional consultation. I stress the counseling aspect here only because my primary concern in this book deals with that aspect of ministry.

Another dimension of this implication which relates to the necessity for consultation is the need for the pastor to have a pastor. Nothing is more destructive than for the minister to assume that while his/her people certainly need pastoral care and counseling, s/he is able to resolve all his/her personal distresses and tensions without help. Ordinarily this assumption takes the form of believing that if one continues in a "close relationship with God," then all the problems of life will be overcome. Ironically, many ministers who might chide parishioners for attempting to go it alone feel that their status as persons of the cloth somehow puts them in a separate category. At the deepest level, there is often the nagging notion that it is a disgrace or an evidence of a lack of faith for a person who is ordained to need help from some other person.

Theologically speaking, such a notion is idolatrous. The idea that ordination removes any person from dependence on the corporate body of believers is false on its face. It tends to persist, however, partially because of the resistance to being found which we have discussed in various dimensions while thinking of the distress of parishioners. From a biblical point of view, it is certain that we can only love as we have been loved, that we can give only as we have received. The fact is that only the minister who has experienced pastoral care is able to function in a pastoral situation.

The problem is a difficult one since we have made little provision for the pastoral care of pastors. Those communions which include bishops assume theoretically that the *pastor pastorum* system can function through the structure. The fact is, however, that the administrative responsibility of persons in the hierarchial system usually becomes a barrier for the parish clergy in sharing the deep problems of life. The same is true of executives in nonhierarchial structures. Where, then, is the pastor to find a pastor? The answer is not simple, and no one solution will fit all situations. It often happens that an older minister in the community will be identified as one to whom ministerial distresses may be brought. More likely, some sort of group experience provides opportunity for dealing with the inner tensions of life. In many urban communities, church-related pastoral counseling centers are now providing pastoral care programs for church professionals and their families financed in whole or in part by denominational budgets. Whatever the form, it is certain that unless and until provision is afforded to pastors for their own pastoral care, the ministry of the church will be less than effective. Here, ministry "outside the walls" is undertaken, born in controversy and in crisis intervention.

## III

We come now to a consideration of the working out of this theme in actual pastoral situations. Here, the situations are a bit different from those set forth in earlier chapters. There, we have seen resistance and rebuff from persons who in some sense or other did identify themselves as wanting or needing help of some sort, even when they presented the matter as "someone else's fault" as in the family situations. Even there, there was the subtle awareness that at least a part of the problem was within, however much the overt focus was external.

### A

The first situation involves a conversation between the minister and an elder who opposes the church's involvement in an interdenominational program in the inner city which attempts to work with young persons who have been in trouble with the law for varieties of reasons, ordinarily having to do with drug abuse. Four churches in the vicinity have worked out a plan to rent an abandoned church building in a transition area of the city where low-income families live in minimum or substandard housing. The issues have been debated widely, and each church has voted through its appropriate channels to participate. An executive committee together with advisory personnel has been appointed, a lease taken on the facility, and a director employed.

The plans have not met with complete approval. Some have opposed the program on the grounds that it would prove too costly, and that the money had better be spent in projects more closely related to the "primary work of the church." Others have felt that, while the idea had merit, the emphases of those in charge of developing the plans was not "spiritual enough," in that it seemed that primary attention would be given not to pressing for conversion but rather toward rehabilitation through work-release opportunities, remedial education classes, and group interaction for personal growth and maturity.

As plans moved on apace, the pastor of one of the churches that had committed itself heavily in financial support as well as in the supplying of volunteers was well aware of the intensity of some of the opposition. Although he had, as he put it, tried in the debates to listen to all sides, he had made no effort to hide his positive feeling about the enterprise. At this juncture, word reached him that one of the elders was not only opposed to the entire undertaking, but was about to mount a campaign not only to rescind the church's action in approving the work but also to attempt to bring about his resignation.

205

Upon hearing of this reported effort, he called the elder at his office, and asked if he could come to see him in the next day or two. At first the elder indicated that he did not see any particular matter that they could discuss profitably; however, with some reluctance, he agreed to a meeting the following afternoon at two o'clock. In the conversation that follows, E = Elder, M = Minister.

1. M.     *(Entering the elder's office, having been announced by secretary.)* Joe, I appreciate your letting me come. This is not an easy time for you or for me . . .

2. E.     Well, that's an understatement! Please sit down.

3. M.     The occasion for my coming is that word has reached me that you want to rescind our action and want my resignation. . . . I'm not much inclined to give credence to rumors, and wanted to find out from you just what is happening.

4. E.     Well, there's no need for me to beat around the bush with you, Reverend. What you heard is, in effect, just what I intend, and neither you nor anyone else can stop me. I still am bewildered and puzzled why you hatched out this scheme and kept pushing it even when you saw how controversial it had become. I should think that your vow to maintain the "peace and purity of the church" would mean more to you than it obviously does!

In the opening part of this conversation the issues are set forth clearly. The minister's definition of his being there (3 M) is an open statement of fact as he sees it, and an invitation to the elder to clarify the matter in the event that the perception is in error. In addition, the minister's verbalizing of the pain that is real to both of them (1 M) is a simple recognition that whatever happens will hurt. The conversation continues:

5. M.    I appreciate your clarifying your own position, Joe, although in all honesty I do not like for us to be on opposite sides of this matter. In regard to the "peace and purity of the church," I believe very much in my vows, although it is evident you and I do not understand the phrase in the same way, and you resent deeply what I've tried to do . . .

6. E.    Yes, I do. . . . I don't have to remind you that when you came here I was one of your most faithful supporters. Although I was not on the committee, I conferred with them and urged them to recommend you for the job. I never thought you'd do anything like this . . .

7. M.    I do know of your support, and I value it very much. And now what I hear is disappointment, that somehow I've let you down . . .

8. E.    There's no "somehow" to it! You have! The idea of our pouring money down this hair-brained rat hole is absolutely beyond comprehension. There are already too many social agencies to work with these long-hair drug addicts. And now we get into the business of coddling them. That's one of the things that's wrong with our country right now! We've gone too soft on people who

> break the law and tied the hands of police
> and judges. A lot more crack-down and a lot
> less wrist-slapping would put the fear of the
> Lord in those punks!

In both 5 and 7 the minister attempted to define his own perception, and then return to the elder's frame of reference. This type of encounter, as has been noted in earlier chapters, is saying "Here I am, and there you are, and I love you." While the exact words of the minister might have been a bit different in each statement, the fact that he did not condemn the elder or retreat from his own position constitutes the kind of approach that makes reconciliation possible even though it does not assure that it will come.

In retrospect, it was evident that the elder was at the time unable to move beyond a categorical stance with regard to the young people whose difficulties were the occasion for the program of restitution. The references to "long hair," "drug addicts," and "punks" are tangible indices that he cannot allow himself to understand some of their pain and struggle. It is to the minister's credit that he did not make use of this kind of evaluative observation to point out that Jesus found himself confronted with similar hostile opposition when he befriended the harlots, Publicans, and sinners. The minister hoped that the time would come when he and the elder could wrestle creatively with the fact that "those who are well have no need for a physician, but those who are sick" (Matt. 9:12). In both 6 and 8, the elder verbalized his disappointment, his hurt, his resentment and bitterness. The difficult aspect for the minister was to keep in focus the fact that there was in this verbalization the evidence of need for healing and forgiveness, difficult precisely because thus far the elder had given no indication of awareness of or desire to deal with his own situation. The parallel between the attitude of the elder brother on the occasion of his father's welcoming the prodigal is evident. And it is instructive for the minister to recall that while the father did not condemn the elder brother, he also did not negate his love and concern for the prodigal (Luke 15:25-32). The conversation continues:

9. M.   Joe, after I've talked with these young people, it's hard for me to think of them as "punks." Of course they have done all manner of despicable things, none of which I approve! And yet, we can't let them just be thrown on the trash heap. I'm against what they have done and are doing, but I surely want to try to be for them. . . . And . . .

10. E.   I've heard all that spineless syrup before. . . . When they've paid their debt to society, then they can come out; I don't want them on the street where my teen-age daughters have to walk. It's just not safe around here, anymore; and you're going to have them congregating around this church at all hours of day and night . . .

11. M.   I hope many of them will come here; it's been a long time since most of them were near a church. . . . But the very thought of that really cuts you to the quick . . .

12. E.   It surely does! Understand, Reverend, I'm not saying we ought to be cruel to them. . . . But they've got to know that other people have rights, and the world doesn't run just for them!

In 10 the elder reveals some of the basis for his fear and rage. The matter is not academic for him; he has two daughters, and he worries about them as a father. The minister's statement in 9 tends to be somewhat condescending if not condemning, and the reply of the elder in defense indicates that he has sensed the rejection. It may be that the minister had intended to return to the elder's frame of reference and was interrupted, although he does not say this in the verbatim reconstruction. It is, however, commendable that in 11 he does move toward standing with the elder in his hurt, even when he does not agree. And the tone of 12 is just a shadow toward moving away from the violent rejection of earlier statements, even though it is clear that the elder is not near relinquishing his stand on right and justice. The conversation continues:

13. M.      I can certainly agree with that. Maybe the way they come to this sense of responsibility is where you and I differ. I hope that is going to happen at the Youth Center, but . . .

14. E.      (*Interrupting.*) There you go again, back to that hair-brained idea of yours. . . . I don't really think we've got any more to say to each other. . . . And I'm busy, today . . .

15. M.      Well, I believe we have a lot more to say, but this is probably not the time. . . . I'll call you later if that is convenient . . .

16. E.      Very well. Good day.

17. M.      Good day, Joe. God bless you . . .

In presenting this verbatim reconstruction for discussion by colleagues, the minister noted that he had had considerable time to reflect on what had happened.

While he wished that he had been able to facilitate a more constructive interchange between himself and the elder, he was aware that this was not something he could do alone. His "knocking on the door" from time to time in his empathic responses indicated his willingness to "come in" if the door was opened. The slight indication of this possibility in 12 soon passed, and by 14 the door was slammed shut. The minister's closing words were designed to keep the channels of communication open from his perspective. Whether or not the next conversation, in the event that it did occur, would be any more creative there was no way to tell.

It is apparent to anyone who has been in this type of situation that the kind of retrospective analysis that is possible in this discussion is one thing; but to put such into practice in the give and take of the encounter is quite another. The fact is, the minister did remarkably well under the circumstances when the negative factors he might have pursued are contemplated. A bickering argument, a probing for data, an expression of righteous indignation, a condemning denunciation are all illustrative of the many ways the minister might have taken rather than keep the pastoral perspective in focus even as he and the parishioner disagreed.

As to the future, it remains unclear. It is certain that the elder can in fact cause great damage to the minister and might be successful in undermining the youth program. The kinds of questions that inevitably arise include: Did I respond to him in the most helpful way? What aspects of the program am I overlooking in my desire that it be accomplished? Should I try to rally some support in light of his threat that I should resign? It is in dealing with such questions that the minister's relationship to colleagues is invaluable. He relies on them, not to take his side or even to provide the "correct answers" for the next encounter. Rather, in their discussion, he has the opportunity to be delivered from narrow subjectivism and respond to the persons involved in a constructive fashion whatever the outcome. The going "outside the walls" is by definition risky; yet the elder is no less a parishioner because of his position. Indeed, it is in light of his position that who he is as a parishioner with needs becomes quite clear. The only question for the minister is whether or not he will be able to meet those needs in a healing manner.

## B

The second pastoral relationship that helps us understand something of the risk in going outside the walls begins with a phone call to the minister about 8:30 in the evening. She had just come in from a dinner meeting and heard the ring as she entered the house: S = Sam, the husband, J = Jane, the wife; and P = the minister:

1.P.     Hello; this is Barbara Simpson . . .

2.S.     Ms. Simpson, can you talk with me just a little. . . . I need to talk with someone . . . can you . . .

3.P.     Why, yes . . . yes . . . I can't place your voice . . .

4.S.     It's Sam . . . Sam Willis. I think I'm going crazy . . .

5.P.     I'm here, Sam. . . . Can you tell me what's happening . . .

6.S.     It's, uh . . . Oh, Ms. Simpson, Jane's old boyfriend showed up this afternoon, and I got mad, and we had a terrible fight, and she's locked in the bathroom and won't talk with me, and I'm going crazy. . . . What can I do?

7. P.        Sam, I'm on my way. . . . Wait there for me, will you?

8. S.        Yes . . . Yes . . . Hurry!

The minister hung up the phone and raced for her car. Sam and Jane, a seemingly pleasant young couple who had moved to town recently, had visited the church on several occasions. When she had called on them, everything seemed quite appropriate on the surface. They had met in college, both worked, and they had no children. Beyond that, she knew very little.

The porch light was on as she rang the door-bell.

9. S.        Come in . . . come in . . . Please do something. . . . I didn't mean to say what I said. . . . Go talk to her, please . . .

10. P.       I'll go in a minute, Sam. Right now, I need to understand a little better where you are and what's happening to you . . .

This kind of crisis situation is filled with danger for the minister as well as for the parishioner. Being perceived in the role of one who can rectify the situation by "bringing someone around" means that the minister may deal with superficialities but overlook the basic difficulty. All to many ministers in similar situations have gone to plead with the offended spouse, prevailed on him or her to "come back in the room," and after having both promise that they will work things out, have left. To be sure, such a process includes more than what has just been stated, but the essence is not basically different. Ms. Simpson knew that in crisis ministry there is need to deal with the present problem, however defined, including manipulation of the circumstances if necessary. But she was also

aware of the fact that such activity simply buys time
wherein healing can occur, and is not the healing in and of
itself. Simply bringing Jane back into the room might
alleviate the overt separation, but at the expense of true
reconciliation. It was in this sense that she spoke to Sam,
who had indicated by his call a need for help. The
conversation continues:

11. S.    I don't know . . . I really *don't know*. . . . I
          knew about Phil, but seeing him here just
          made me explode. . . . Jane says I am
          unreasonable, and I guess she's right. What
          scares me is that I pushed her around, pretty
          rough . . . and I can't blame her for not
          coming out. . . . Will you ask her . . . please
          . . .

12. P.    I think so. . . . Maybe you and I together
          can do it. . . . I can hear your fear and
          remorse. . . . You really didn't know all that
          anger and resentment was in you . . .

13. S.    No . . . No, I didn't; although I've had a bad
          temper, here of late I've been doing much
          better. . . . To think I would hurt Jane . . .

They talked for about fifteen minutes, and then Ms.
Simpson suggested that they go and speak to Jane. She
realized that Sam truly wanted her to resolve the matter,
and she was willing to do so, if need be; at the same time,
she hoped to involve him in the process as much as
possible from the start. Together, they stood outside the
door to the bathroom:

14. P.    Jane, it's Barbara Simpson from the church;
          Sam called me and I'd like to speak to the

two of you together . . .

15. J.   Go away! And you can take Sam with you, for all I care!

16. P.   I'll go away in a little while; right now I wish you'd come out so we can look at each other as we talk. I'm not at all sure of what's going on in you, and I'd like to know . . .

17. J.   Will you stay with us if I come out, I mean at least until we both calm down just a little . . .

18. P.   Yes, I will. . . . It feels good to me that you are at least partly willing to join us; and also, somewhat uneasy, too, I guess . . .

Jane opened the door, and the three of them went back into the den. The words that followed were in some sense predictable. Sam continued to express remorse and promised that he would never again do such a thing. Jane was quite skeptical, not sure that she could ever trust him again. The minister attempted to listen to and support both of them without taking sides, even though both tried in subtle and not so subtle fashion to make her an ally against the other. After about forty-five minutes, she left, having made an appointment for both of them to come to her study the following evening.

As she returned home, she had a sense of satisfaction in being a part of the process of reconciliation in the marriage of Sam and Jane. At the same time, she was quite aware of the pain and struggle that lay ahead, both for them and for her as she walked with them through the dark places brought in part to the surface by the crisis of this day. It is to her credit that she resisted the temptation to allow herself to be lulled into the illusion that she had "helped" them, and that they were now all right. Deep within, she knew that going outside the walls involved far more than such temporary relief. As she turned off the light, she found herself grateful both for the start, and for the opportunity to engage Sam and Jane as their marriage emerged from the crucible of commitment and covenant.

## C

This final situation is fraught with danger of quite a different sort than that encountered by Barbara Simpson and the minister's conversation with the elder. The notes that follow are reproduced essentially as they were presented by the minister who brought the matter for discussion by his consultation group.

I was awakened by the phone and as I turned on the light saw that it was about 2:45 A.M. The voice on the other end was tense and frightened. She identified herself as the "proprietor" of a house on East 11th Street, and wondered if I would come as soon as I could. One of the "visitors" had become very agitated, seemed to be alternately suicidal and homicidal and was apparently asking for me. As best as she could gather, he had met me when I had participated in a discussion at an A.A. meeting. Now, although he had been drinking, he was not drunk, but seemed to be bordering on hysteria. Sometimes cursing, sometimes crying, he said he was no good, that he was damned, and that he needed to see the preacher. "For God's sake, get him here as soon as you can!"

Try as I would, I couldn't place him. I asked for the exact address and said that I would be there within twenty minutes. As I pulled on my clothes and drove through the deserted streets, I reflected on my decision to go. To say that I was afraid would be an understatement! I had no idea what I would find, whether he would be violent, what I could possibly do that would be helpful. Should I call someone to go with me, even if only to sit in the car while I went in? Should I call a friend of mine who worked the night desk at the police station?

Besides the fear of what I would find inside once I got there was the realization that if I was seen in that neighborhood and going into that house in the early hours of the morning my behavior would be subject to all manner of misinterpretation. Since I had been in the community only a little over a year, I wondered whether I had established the kind of reputation which would enable people to know that if I went there it was for ministry and not for mischief. Fleetingly, I was envious of my physician friends, whose mission of healing found cultural approval wherever it led. By now I was in the block; still time to turn back. I walked up the steps and rang the bell.

The woman who met me had a face that was lined and seemed hard; but there was a softness in her eyes. "Thank you for coming," she said. "He's upstairs." Our steps made little sound on the faded carpet, and by the time we passed the turn on the landing, I could hear the man. There was a tightness in my throat as she opened the door after a brief knock. He was lying on the bed, wide-eyed, groaning, "O God, O God, Ooooh God!" There was a young woman sitting in a straight chair trying to calm him. "Now, then; now, now . . . don't take on so . . . it'll be all right . . ."

"The preacher's here," said my guide. I walked over to the bed, and sat gently on the edge beside him. "I'm here," I said; and he grabbed my hand in a viselike grip. The young girl and the woman backed out of the doorway, saying, "We'll be right out here if you need us."

The primary questions for consideration in the discussion by the support group turned on the propriety of going alone in answer to the call and the nature of the pastoral care of the person in distress, including follow-up. For our purpose here, only the first is considered.

There was not a unanimity in the judgment of the group regarding the appropriateness of the minister's going on his own. Several voiced the opinion that while it might have represented a certain amount of courage, it also might have been short-sighted, and somewhat irresponsible. As one member put it, "If you are going into turbulent waters to rescue a drowning person, the presence of a back-up person is highly desirable; and in any event, some sort of rope or life-preserver may mean that both of you come through the experience alive. It may be heroic to drown with the victim, but how much better to be sure you have taken every precaution to rescue him." Others demurred, taking the position that to call the police or even to have a friend sitting in the car would have been to inject a factor into the situation that might make reconciliation more difficult.

From a different perspective, i.e., the standpoint of the reputation of the minister, several noted that there was the necessity not only to avoid evil, but also to avoid the appearance of evil. In expanding on this factor, the point was made that while misunderstanding is certain to arise even under the best of circumstances, there is need to give as clear signals as possible regarding one's own character and intent. Others called attention to the fact that Jesus' reputation as a glutton and a wine-bibber, a friend of sinners seemed to imply that one did what seemed best and let the reputation chips fall where they may.

The conclusion of the discussion moved away from the rightness or wrongness of this or that behavior to what the behavior meant to the minister. Here, on more solid ground, the focus was on whether the decision was the most appropriate, taking into account the pastor's responsibility not only to the man in distress but also to members of his congregation and the community as a whole. Recognizing the inevitable ambiguity in whatever was decided, the criterion most applicable was the question of whether or not the minister was attempting to prove something to himself, or was acting in the best interests of those for whom he had assumed a responsibility. Couched in these terms, the conversation provided a means whereby the minister could examine in a clearer light his own motives and thus both look critically at what was done and find a firmer basis for creative pastoral care in future situations of crisis. On this foundation, he was better able to run the legitimate risks of redemptive relationships and avoid irresponsible risks not inherent in the pastoral task.

## IV

Risk and redemption is a theme that permeates all pastoral counseling. It is, perhaps, the most difficult aspect confronting the minister who wishes to provide the means for creative living among those whose lives are involved in his own. We tend to become glib in using the biblical language that deals with sacrifice, of taking up the cross, of laying down one's life for others. Perhaps nowhere do these words bite deeper into the heart of the minister than in his/her counseling relationships, his/her entering into the hurt and loneliness, the resentment and bitterness that mark the hiding of the person whose fear erects the barriers of separation. By the same token, perhaps nowhere is there more occasion for genuine satisfaction and rejoicing than when the person who is lost and lonely is able to be found and restored to the fullness of life that is possible through the good news of reconciliation and redemption. Then it is that the risk is seen as truly worthwhile and, in the words of Jesus, there is "joy in heaven . . . before the angels of God" (Luke 15:7, 10).

# *Epilogue*

We began by raising the question of whether or not the Bible has anything to say to the minister who engages in pastoral counseling, and the thrust of the discussion has been not only to answer the question in the affirmative, but also to demonstrate the way in which biblical data are relevant for informing the work of the pastor. It is my hope that what has been said both theoretically and illustratively is of value to the reader in considering day-to-day procedures in the care of souls.

Nevertheless, as always, I come to the conclusion of the work with certain ambiguities stemming principally from the limitations of the printed page to provide an adequate medium for dialogue. Again and again I have wished it might be possible to discuss the concepts in a face-to-face fashion. That the biblical themes are constructive means for my own understanding of the relationship between the Bible and pastoral counseling is certainly real to me. Whether this presentation has made it possible for the reader to wrestle with the data and on the basis of that wrestling to find deeper avenues into an understanding of the pastoral task is not as clear. The two pitfalls that I trust can be avoided are rejection of the ideas out of hand or the acceptance of them uncritically.

So it is that I like to believe that the reader will, at this point, look back over the discussion as a whole. This retrospective examination of the overall issue can provide a context that is helpful. The procedure of identifying subthemes and examining process from various perspectives has the advantage of closer scrutiny. At the same time, such an approach runs the risk of distortion in that the whole may be lost while considering the parts. Thus the opportunity for overall reflection provides a means for perceiving the significance of the several foci.

If, as I indicated in the Preface, this discussion proves to be a stimulus to others to press for further clarification and elucidation, then all of us will be able to function more effectively in pastoral ministry. This is possible, as I see it, only when the reader moves beyond the point of agreement or disagreement toward a more penetrating exploration of the biblical implications for pastoral counseling.

Toward this end, I have one concluding word. For reasons of space limitations as noted in chaper 1, I have developed only five themes. And I also stated my belief that there are many others that should prove of great benefit in this enterprise. I think of the "significance of name" as helping us deal with the whole matter of identity. From the naming of the animals in Genesis 2 to the hosts of Revelation whose names are written in the Book of Life, this theme moves across almost every page of the biblical material. As Abram becomes Abraham; Sarai, Sarah; Jacob, Israel, we perceive the significance of newness of life and true identity. The awesome power of name is seen in the refusal of the Lord to place himself at Moses' disposal on the back side of Horeb, and his unwillingness to reveal his name to Jacob at Jabbok. In this context, the revealing of the name of Jesus as Savior, Messiah, Emmanuel, describes the wonder and grace of the Incarnation, since now he will be vulnerable to the hurts of mankind. And it is in his Name that the disciples discover the power that transforms their own lives.

Another theme that pervades the pages of biblical material can best be described by the term "dependence and independence." Illustrated most often in parent-child relationships, it sheds light on the whole matter of authority. The struggle for maturity, the reaction to reality, the experiencing of inner creativity all find roots in this theme. Authority too quickly accepted or too long resisted provides a clue to the nature of hiding and movement toward life. In this context, the relationship of the pastor and the parishioner(s) can be assessed on a constructive level in terms of the process of healing.

Still another theme is characterized by the notion of "individuality and community." Although aspects of this theme are found in "conformity and rebellion," there are here dimensions that open the way for evaluating pastoral care in one-to-one settings, in families, and in groups. Such an exploration provides contextual referents for assessing the matter of space and distance, the necessity for corporate as well as personal involvement.

There are others; but this is enough to demonstrate that any list is suggestive not exhaustive. If, in the days to come, there are persons who are willing to delve more deeply into the matter of biblical data for pastoral counseling, we shall be the richer for it. We have come a long way in understanding the healing process, but there are few who would hold that we have little more than scratched the surface. Any word that enhances our capacity to communicate the good news of reconciliation will bring us closer to fulfilling the ministry to which we are committed.

# Notes

## 1. The Bible and Pastoral Care and Counseling

1. The essential argument of the first two sections of this chapter draws on two of my articles published in *Interpretation*. Cf. "Pastoral Care and Counseling in Biblical Perspective," 27:307-26, and "Implications of Anthropology for Pastoral Care and Counseling," 33:156-71.

2. "*What* I say to a man on his deathbed is a holy matter; but it is a matter no less holy *how* I am to say it to him in such a way that he shall understand and appreciate it. A person might—to put it somewhat strongly—go to heaven on account of the *what* but go to hell on account of the *how*. To despise the question of the *how* is a sign, not of theological seriousness, but of theological intellectualism. The *what* is, as it were, guarded by faith, but the *how* has to be guarded by love. But where the *how*, and therefore love is lacking, there faith must be lacking also." Emil Brunner, *Natural Theology* (London: Geoffrey Bles, The Century Press, 1946), pp. 57 ff.

3. John T. McNeill, *A History of the Cure of Souls* (New York: Harper, 1951). See also H. Richard Niebuhr, ed., *The Ministry in Historical Perspectives* (Harper, 1956); William A. Clebsch and Charles R. Jaekel, *Pastoral Care in Historical Perspective* (Englewood Cliffs, N.J.: Prentice-Hall, 1964); C. W. Brister, *Pastoral Care in the Church* (Harper, 1964, 1977).

4. What follows, and indeed the entire argument of the book, is based on the conviction that the Bible is authoritative in matters of faith and practice. It is beyond the scope of this discussion to go into

all the ramifications of biblical authority. A constructive treatment is found in John Bright, *The Authority of the Old Testament* (Nashville: Abingdon, 1967). Other works include C. H. Dodd, *The Authority of the Bible* (New York: Harper Torchbooks, 1938); D. E. Nineham, ed., *The Church's Use of the Bible, Past and Present* (London: S.P.C.K., 1963); J. K. S. Reid, *The Authority of Scripture* (London: Methuen & Co., 1957); and Robert W. Jenson, "On the Problem(s) of Scriptural Authority," *Interpretation,* July, 1977, pp. 237-50. I am not using the term "authority" in the sense of some sort of rigid and inflexible power that coerces obedience. Rather, I understand the Bible as the source to which we turn as theologians for an understanding of the true meaning of our life and work in the belief that God who is the ultimate source of all authority reveals himself through the Scriptures. (Cf. Bright's discussion of the "normative" use of the Bible [*The Authority of the Old Testament,* pp. 28 ff.])

5. This is not said with the intent to be critical of students and ministers. Their learning experiences have, by and large, been informed by the cultural patterns of counseling and therapy, and it is to be expected that these presuppositions would be incorporated in their own attempts to be of help. Most of the widely used books in pastoral counseling are rooted in the behavioral sciences and tend to be oriented toward insight or behavioral goals. While the Bible is often cited as supporting the necessity for the cure of souls, it is rare when it is employed to inform process. An exception is the work of Jay Adams, who finds in the Greek word *nouthesis* (Col. 3:16; Rom. 15:14; Acts 20:31; and others) a basis for behavior modification as the essence of the pastoral counseling task. He is convinced that right "doing" is the key to right "being," and his aim is "straightening out the individual by changing his patterns of behavior to conform to biblical standards." Cf. Jay E. Adams, *Competent To Counsel* (Grand Rapids: Baker Book House, 1970), p. 46.

6. *Westminster Confession of Faith,* chap. 1; *Westminster Larger Catechism,* #3; *Westminster Shorter Catechism,* #3.

7. The same is true in other functions of ministry as well. It is

obvious that drawing on biblical "sermons" as norms for homiletical practice leads inevitably to the conclusion that the appropriate length for a sermon should not exceed three or four minutes, since by and large all "sermons" recorded in the New Testament can be delivered in approximately that time or less. Cf. Acts 2:14-36; 3:12-26; 10:34-43; 13:16-41; 17:22-31; and others. However much some in the congregation might approve of such an arrangement, the minister knows that this is not the correct remedy for sermonic boredom!

8. Most of us have smiled as we heard persons say that they sought divine guidance in naming a child by opening the Bible at a random page and using the first word upon which their eyes fell as the appropriate answer. My mother tells of a lad in her school class whose name, "Page 144," was derived in such a fashion! Much more serious have been the consequences of asking the early chapters of Genesis to answer our questions on geological formation or the passage of time, which questions are inappropriate to the meaning and intent of the passages.

9. Cf. *Interpretation,* 27:321 ff. for a more extensive statement of the line of thought developed here.

10. Cf. Augustine's *Credo ut intelligam.* He wrote: "Understanding is the reward of faith. Therefore seek not to understand that thou mayest believe, but believe that thou mayest understand." In Johann. Evang. XXIX, 6X, Thomas A. Doegege calls attention to the relationship between *notitia, assensus,* and *fiducia* in "A Developmental View of Faith," *Journal of Religion and Health,* Oct., 1972, 2:31.

11. For a provocative study of punishment and restoration see W. Sibley Towner, *How God Deals with Evil* (Philadelphia: Westminster Press, 1976). Towner's position is that there are two distinct strands in Scripture, one based on *lex talionis* in which God punishes those who err, the other based on God's redeeming purpose in which God comes to restore those who err.

12. Cf. *inter alia,* Rom. 3:21-26; Eph. 2:8-10.

13. Cf. also John 3:1 ff.

14. Deut. 6:6-9, 20 ff. Cf. also Deut. 11:13; 13:13, and so on.

15. This priority is always evident in the Pauline Epistles. The suggestions for living follow the affirmation of God's grace ratner than produce it. One of the difficulties we face is beginning at, e.g., Romans 12 or Ephesians 4 without taking into account the transformation that makes such words possible as set forth in the chapters preceding the admonitions.

16. The story of the good Samaritan is a case in point. The answer of the lawyer is correct; the ironic and tragic aspect is that there is no way he or any one of us can possibly love the Lord our God with all our heart and our neighbor as ourselves. It is this realistic factor which helps us understand the purpose of the story of Mary and Martha, which follows the good Samaritan—i.e., Mary, who sits at Jesus' feet, rather than Martha, the "doer," receives the blessing. Cf. Luke 10:25-42.

17. This basic theme begins in the Yahwist primeval history. "To begin with, the pattern of Gen. 2–3 is not unfamiliar. It has four parts: God's goodness, man's revolt, divine punishment, divine forgiveness. The same pattern recurs in the following stories of the primeval history and in the national history as well, especially in Ex. 14-16; 32-34; and Num. 10-21 passim." Peter Ellis, *The Yahwist: The Bible's First Theologian* (Collegeville, Minn.: Liturgical Press, 1968), p. 185.

18. Westminster Confession of Faith, I, 9.

19. We have come a long way since the days when the unity of the Bible as "salvation history" seemed to be the last word in biblical interpretation and understanding. A good discussion of the weaknesses of this sort of approach is Brevard Childs' *Biblical Theology in Crisis* (Philadelphia: Westminster Press, 1970). Childs traces the course of the waxing and waning of this and other aspects of "biblical Theology."

20. *Cf. Towner, How God Deals with Evil*, esp. pp. 142 ff.

21. Cf. my "Implications of Anthropology for Pastoral Care and Counseling," *Interpretation*, 33:163 ff.

22. *Ibid.*, p. 162.

23. *Gerhard von Rad, The Problem of the Hexateuch*, trans. E. W. Trumann (Edinburgh: Oliver & Boyd, 1965), first published as

*Gesammelte Studien zum Alten Testament* (Munich: Kaiser Verlag, 1938); Martin Noth, *A History of Pentateuchal Traditions*, trans. Bernard Anderson (Englewood Cliffs, N.J.: Prentice-Hall, 1972), first published as *Überlieferungsgeschichte des Pentateuch* (Stuttgart: W. Kohlhammer, 1948); John Bright, *The Authority of the Bible* (Nashville: Abingdon, 1967); Walter Eichrodt, *Theology of the Old Testament*, trans J. A. Baker (Philadelphia: Westminster Press, 1961), first published as *Theologie des Alten Testaments* (Leipzig: J. C. Hinrichs, 1933).

24. "Noth emphasizes the original cultic independence of the various themes. . . . Nevertheless, these single themes themselves always presuppose the idea of the whole." *Old Testament Theology*, vol. I, trans. D. M. G. Stalker (Edinburgh: Oliver & Boyd, 1962), first published as *Theologie des Alten Testaments* (Munich: Kaiser Verlag, 1957), p. 122 n. Bright, *The Authority of the Bible*, also sees the themes interrelated and inherent in all of Scripture.

25. "Here [in the Yahwist's material] we have before us, in magnificent style, the oldest literary composition of the oldest traditions of Israel. It has determined to a great extent the outline and theme of the present-day Pentateuch, the Torah, as the basic canon. 'It may be said without exaggeration that, of all the Pentateuchal narrative sets forth, it contains what is of greatest moment theologically.' " Hans Walter Wolff, "The Kerygma of the Yahwist," trans. Wilbur A. Benware, *Interpretation*, 20:132. (The concluding quotation is from Martin Noth, *Überlieferungsgeschichte des Pentateuch*, 1948, p. 256.)

26. *Genesis*, trans. John H. Marks (Philadelphia: Westminster Press, 1961); first published as *Das Erste Buch Mose, Genesis* (Göttingen: Vandenhoeck & Ruprescht, 1956). Cf. also: "His [J's] touch is singularly light: with a few strokes he paints a scene which, before he has finished, is impressed indelibly upon his reader's memory. In ease and grace his narratives are unsurpassed; everything is told with precisely the amount of detail that is required; the narrative never lingers, and the reader's interest is sustained to the end." (S. R. Driver, *An Introduction to the*

*Literature of the Old Testament,* p. 119.) Also: "What is truly distinctive about this writer [J] is his incisive style, his economy and boldness of presentation, his insight into human nature, and the recognition that a higher order and purpose may lie behind seemingly incomprehensible human events. There is common agreement that we have in J . . . not only the most gifted writer, but one of the greatest figures in world literature." (E. Speiser, Anchor Bible *Genesis,* p. xxvii.) Both latter quotations are from Ellis, *The Yahwist,* p. 22 n. Whether the Yahwist material was the work of one specific person or several is a question not germane to this study.

27. For a provocative study of the Yahwist, see Ellis, *The Yahwist: The Bible's First Theologian.*

28. The "atypical" dimension of pastoral counseling is seen in the scheduling of regular weekly sessions consisting of purposefully limited duration, i.e., fifty-five minutes, to continue over an indefinite series of sessions until the parishioner(s) can function without such an arrangement.

29. A similar figure that helps to distinguish between pastoral counseling and pastoral care can be seen in dealing with a plant that, for whatever reason, is taken or torn out of the ground and has its roots exposed. Some sort of emergency measure is essential—water, a covering of the roots with burlap or earth—until such time as the plant is again firmly set in the ground where the life-giving resources can be tapped through ordinary procedures.

30. In the same fashion, there was a time in my earlier ministry when I saw husbands and wives separately for the most part. While there were occasions of genuine growth, I now find it much more constructive to see these persons together as the three of us move toward new patterns of relating emerging from the crucible of the relationship in the encounter of the counseling sessions.

31. The literature on family systems and family therapy is now extensive, and every minister can profit from a study of these researches. The titles listed here are suggestive rather than comprehensive, designed to assist those who would like an introduction to family systems and family therapy. Nat Ackerman,

*The Psychodynamics of Family Life* (New York: Basic Books, 1958); Donald Block, ed., *Techniques of Family Psychotherapy, A Primer* (New York: Grune and Stratton, 1973); Murray Bowen, *Family Therapy in Clinical Practice* (New York: Aronson, 1978); Philip Guerin, *Family Therapy, Theory and Practice* (New York: Gardner, 1976); Salvador Minuchin, *Families and Family Therapy* (Cambridge: Harvard University Press, 1974); Virginia Satir, *Conjoint Family Therapy* (Palo Alto: Science and Behavior Books, 1967); W. Toman, *Family Constellation* (New York: Springer Verlag, 1969). See also A. J. Van den Blink, "Family Therapy and Pastoral Care," *The Journal of Pastoral Care*, September 1974, pp. 183-98.

## 2. Initiative and Freedom

1. "The creation of man as described by the Yahwist expresses an understanding of humans as creatures that has been almost completely lost in Christian theology. Humans simply existing as separate individuals are not the creatures intended by God." Claus Westermann, *What Does the Old Testament Say About God?* (Atlanta: John Knox Press, 1979), p. 41. Gen. 2:18 is better understood if read, "It is impossible for the man to live alone." Cf. *inter alia*, U. Cassuto, *A Commentary on the Book of Genesis*, trans. Israel Abrahams, Part I (Jerusalem: The Magnes Press), pp. 126 ff.

2. Cf. also Gen. 15:18; 17:17, 22, and others. There are, of course, two types of covenant in scriptural materials; namely, election covenants and reciprocal covenants. In the former, God announces a choice as in the case of Abram. Such covenants are made without requiring an identified response. The second type is that represented by Sinai where there exists a reciprocal dimension in the order of a treaty. The emphasis given to the first here underscores the initiative of God where there is response that is made in freedom, a response that is not automatic or even mandatory.

3. Parallel to the concept of covenant as depicting God's initiative in reestablishing the broken relationships is the factor of

election, which moves from the first to the last in the biblical narrative. Seen clearly in the call of Abram, it is reiterated in such passages as Deut. 7:6, "For you are a people holy to the Lord your God; the Lord your God has chosen you to be a people for his own possession." Cf. *inter alia* Deut. 14:2; Ps. 33:12; I Pet. 2:9; Rev. 17:14.

4. George W. Coats, "The God of Death," *Interpretation*, 29:230. Cf. also: "The wheel of history—if the Yahwist's foreshadowing in Gen. 3:15 is to be believed—will eventually return man to the happy state he enjoyed before the fall, but men will turn the wheel themselves, freely and with the help of God's love and the enlightenment of his revelation. . . . Thus, Adam is free. Cain is free. Joseph's sinful brothers are free. The Israelites in the desert are free. Man sins freely throughout the saga, but he also responds freely and it is ultimately through the response of love and fidelity that the Yahwist sees the fulfillment of God's plan." Ellis, *The Yahwist*, p. 160.

5. The term "freedom" is used in the Bible in two related, but distinct, ways. There is the whole concept of human freedom with which we are dealing here. Alongside this there is the freedom of deliverance from sin which comes as a consequence of God's reconciling the world unto himself (II Cor. 5:16-21). This latter usage is set forth in such passages as, "For freedom Christ has set us free" (Gal. 5:1), and "the law of the Spirit of life in Christ Jesus has set me free from the law of sin and death" (Rom. 8:2). Although both impinge directly on the human situation, it is the concept of human freedom seen in wo/man's capacity to say no to God that concerns us as we contemplate the divine initiative and the freedom of wo/man's response. Elsewhere I have discussed in greater detail the concept of freedom in human development. Cf. *With Wings as Eagles* (Nashville: Abingdon, 1979), pp. 93 ff.

6. In the following chapter, we deal more explicitly with the "fear of being found" so evident in this story, and so crucial in the reestablishing of broken relationships. See chapter 3.

7. In looking at the minister's perspective in "Initiative and Freedom," there is no intent to suggest that clergy participate in

only one dimension of the theme, i.e., as initiators, whereas parishioners are solely responders. Thus, the use of the term "minister" for the care provider and the term parishioner(s) for the care receiver is ultimately artificial. No help is ever given without the helper being helped, and vice versa. Only persons who have received pastoral care are able to provide pastoral care. Consequently, while our focus is on the one who functions as pastor to others, the discussion is meaningful only in the context of the wholeness of the theme for all persons, whether pastor or parishioner, whether ordained or lay.

8. Usually when a person says to another, "I have a problem, and I want your help," the person approached is gripped by the inner feeling: "Now *I* have a problem. What am I going to do with *you!*" I have dealt at length with the limitations on the part of the pastor in my *Referral in Pastoral Counseling*, rev. ed. (Nashville: Abingdon, 1978), esp. pp. 29-57.

9. Cf. K. R. Menninger, *Theory of Psychoanalytic Technique* (New York: Basic Books, 1958), for a consideration of what the "party of the first part" and the "party of the second part" agree to give and receive (esp. pp. 15-42).

10. The question regarding initiative in offering help has been highlighted by members of Alcoholics Anonymous who took the position that only as the alcoholic recognized a need for help and asked for it could any constructive action occur. While affirming the validity of this point of view, others argued that there was value in indicating to the alcoholic that help was available if desired, thus in that sense taking the initiative. Theologically, forgiveness comes before confession of need as seen in Christ's word from the cross. See also, John Calvin, *Institutes of the Christian Religion* (Philadelphia: Presbyterian Board of Christian Education), who makes this point. The fact is that until the person sees a way out, there is no possibility of owning the true nature of the problem. This concept is discussed in more detail in *With Wings as Eagles*, pp. 131 ff.

11. The same is true when the parishioner takes the initiative, except that the first definition is made by the parishioner: "I have a

problem, and would like to have your help." The responding definition by the minister either agrees to enter into the contract or declines to do so, for whatever reason.

12. A no does not necessarily imply rejection; it may be that the minister has another appointment soon and, thus, feels it unwise to pursue the matter at that time. In that event, a later meeting is scheduled.

13. Only a sensitivity to the mores of the group and the feelings of the individual can indicate the extent of such a personal source of isolation and disgrace. Thus the minister can never proceed simply on his/her own value judgments if s/he is to participate fully in the life of the parishioner. This does not mean that the minister must alter or abandon his/her own position at any point; it does mean that s/he can never assume that because s/he considers such and such a situation distressing but not disgraceful the parishioner will of necessity share his/her viewpoint. As an illustration of how these matters change, I recall my father stating that when his elder sister contracted TB around the turn of the century, the family felt disgraced. He went on to note how drastically this situation changed in his own lifetime to the place where TB, however unwelcome, was not an occasion for social embarrassment. In like manner, we have witnessed a change in the whole matter of help for those in emotional distress, for persons retarded, and others. As such matters come out in the open and can be dealt with in terms of help rather than with real or assumed censure or disgrace, the notion of bearing one another's burdens takes on new meaning. At the same time, the sense of personal guilt, whether attached to some situation generally considered blameworthy or not, is always to be taken seriously as being a genuine aspect of the person's perception of self in relationship.

14. I have often sat for as long as thirty minutes or more with persons who were silently trying out new feelings about themselves. Such a silence, far from being coercive, is filled with rich meaning. The person will speak when ready. During such silences I usually do not move unless the person shifts position, in

which case I do, also. Direct gaze is avoided lest such eye contact be disruptive for the parishioner.

### 3. Fear and Faith

1. In chapter 5 the Jacob Saga is considered in greater detail as a means for understanding the resistance to healing.

2. Cf. "Implications of Anthropology for Pastoral Care and Counseling," esp. pp. 163, 164.

3. I stress this, perhaps, since it is often difficult for me to remember as I sit with a parishioner in a counseling conversation. A constant reminder to me is the chair in my office at Union Seminary where the parishioner sits. It is disreputable, to say the least, and many former students who read these words will probably smile as they recall its battered condition. It had been abandoned as worthless when I arrived at the seminary in 1952, but since it was in the former dormitory room then assigned to me for an office, I decided to let it stay for awhile. As the years went by, it gradually deteriorated. The slipcover wore thin, fell apart, and now hangs as a kind of tattered "skirt" around the legs of the chair. One arm fell off about 1958, and I patched it up with some wire. The webbing split during the 1960s, but I tacked in some new and got a small cushion to cover the upholstery tacks. In the wooden arm there is a deep groove; it was begun years ago by someone who anxiously ran a thumbnail along the grain making a slight line. Through the years others have retraced this mark until now it is tangible evidence of the inner tension that comes out unconsciously in times of stress. Although for many years I have been in another office with modern furniture, I have kept the old chair as a constant reminder that no one who sits in it wants to be there. It speaks to me of the wretchedness that lies just beneath the facade, and from time to time I sit in the chair so I will never forget what it is like to be on the other side of pastoral counseling.

4. "In sin and salvation alike, individuality is there, however far society or culture may mold us. . . . [Thus] man is never totally victimized by outside forces. His sin is not in what others do to him but in what he *lets* them do to him. Forces outside us can do much

to us without our permission, but there is that which cannot be done apart from our consent or response. You may be able to strike me without my consent or cooperation, but you cannot make me angry or make me hate without some measure of my consent. I am not responsible for what you do to me; I am responsible for what I *let* you do to me. However much another may contribute to my sinning, in the final analysis it is I who sin. . . . It is a part of being human that even in sin I have my measure of identity, freedom, and sovereignty." Frank Stagg, *Polarities of Man's Existence in Biblical Perspective* (Philadelphia: Westminster Press, 1973), p. 77. Stagg goes on to make the same point regarding salvation.

5. An illustration of this process is given in my *With Wings as Eagles*, as Grace speaks with Mary, thus enabling her to respond differently to Frank. See, esp. pp. 86-90, 154-56.

6. From a technical perspective, as noted in chapter 1, a workable distinction between pastoral care and pastoral counseling is that the former is short-range whereas the latter is long-range. The principles with which we are concerned are the same whether the pastoral conversation with the parishioner is a first encounter with no others to follow or, as is true in this situation, the fifteenth or thirtieth meeting. Since, ordinarily, much personal distress tends to be resolved with the passage of time, the usual purpose of pastoral care is to facilitate the resolution so that the parishioner experiences more creative ways of dealing with the ordinary stresses and strains of life through renewed relationships. If, however, this does not occur in a relatively brief space of time, i.e., three or four weeks, then it is certain that the personal distortions are deep-rooted and tangled. It is at that point that the minister makes a decision as to whether it is appropriate to continue seeing the parishioner, or whether a referral is indicated. Most ministers do not have the time or the skill for long-term counseling and rely on colleagues in pastoral-counseling centers or similar endeavors for that type of care. Indeed, apart from a clear understanding of what is happening in the relationship, which requires regular consultation with a knowledgeable colleague, ministers run considerable risk to themselves and their parishioners if they

extend consecutive interviews more than five or six times. The minister in this situation had engaged in graduate study in pastoral counseling and participated regularly in a peer group where consultation was available. For a more detailed discussion on this pastoral limitation, see my *Referral in Pastoral Counseling*, pp. 50 ff.

7. Chapter 6, dealing with the theme "risk and redemption," discusses in more detail the risks of pastoral counseling.

8. The same principle is evident in overt disagreement with the person's behavior when that behavior is perceived as destructive. This point is considered at greater length in chapter 5.

9. Illustrative, among many others, is the Emmaus Road experience. As Jesus took the bread, blessed and broke it, and gave it to them, "their eyes were opened and they recognized him." It was only then that they could "understand" that which they had already heard. "Did not our hearts burn within us while he talked to us on the road, while he opened to us the scriptures" (Luke 24:13-35, esp. vv. 31, 32).

10. "It seems to me to be clear that insofar as Gen. 2–3 is concerned, man stands responsible, fully creature, even in the beginning of the story. There is no suggestion that he realizes his full stature only after his disobedience as if before the fall he existed as half-creature." George W. Coats, "The God of Death," *Interpretation*, 29:230 n.

11. For a discussion of how "faith" becomes "the faith," see *With Wings as Eagles*, esp. pp. 122 ff.

12. This point is discussed at greater length in *Referral in Pastoral Counseling*, pp. 59-86.

### 4. Conformity and Rebellion

1. It is important in our consideration of this theme to recognize at the outset the fact that the typical response of the first, or conformist, type and the second, or rebel, type is not inherent. In the biblical narrative, the first type is ordinarily the firstborn, just as the second type is usually the younger sibling. In most instances the biblical narrative deals only with two siblings, although there

are exceptions. As we watch this pattern worked out in contemporary life, the third child will gradually move toward one or the other general characteristic: in like manner, the fourth, fifth, and so on. On those occasions where the first born rebels, for whatever reason, the second child is much more likely to conform. Thus, "first type" may not refer to the firstborn, although it usually does; in like manner, "second type" may not be the second born. A more detailed discussion of first- and second-type persons is set forth in my *With Wings as Eagles*, esp. pp. 30, 31, 46-53.

2. The archetypal figure of Cain is illustrative of the skill by which the Yahwist material deals with the ancient stories so that what emerges sheds light on human behavior that is comprehensive and universal.

3. As noted, the text gives not the slightest inkling of why one offering was received and the other not received. Biblical interpreters through the years have attempted to explain the distinction by reading into the material that which is not there. Usually, the explanation turns on the blood sacrifice of Abel, but such a meaning is imposed rather than inherent. The focus of the story is Cain's reaction, not the nature of the sacrifice. Cf. Heb. 11:4, which says Abel's sacrifice was more excellent than Cain's, and I John 3:12, which suggests that Cain's deeds were evil; neither implication is in the Genesis text. By the same token, Matt. 23:35 calls Abel "innocent," although there is also no evidence of this in the text. Significantly, Luke omits "innocent" in his rendition of the saying of Jesus (11:51).

4. Cf. Ps. 121:5. A penetrating discussion of this point is given in "Am I My Brother's Keeper?" by Paul Riemann. *Interpretation*, 24:482 ff.

5. Two generations later it is noteworthy that Joseph, a second type, is sold into the hands of the Ishmaelites by his first-type brothers (Gen. 37:25 ff.)

6. The experience of the young businessman in the previous chapter is a classic illustration of the first-type person.

7. The composite Jacob saga is considered in detail as we turn in

the following chapter to a discussion of the theme "death and rebirth."

8. This basic pattern, which eventuates in the younger superseding the elder but only after considerable suffering and anguish, is the more remarkable in the context of the "first born" being "consecrated to the Lord" (Exod. 13:2, 12, 15; Luke 2:23; and others). In addition to the citations already made, we are reminded of Leah and Rachel (Gen. 29 ff.), Zerah and Perez (Gen. 38:27-30), Manasseh and Ephraim (Gen. 48:1-22), Reuben and Judah (Gen. 49:1-12). (It should be noted that although the supplanting sequence in the latter involves Reuben and Judah, it is Joseph who triumphs in the overall story.) It can be argued that this pattern is the Yahwist's way of justifying Solomon's assuming the throne rather than Adonijah (I Kings 1 and 2). While a case can be made for this interpretation, the persistence of the theme beyond the Yahwist material attests that it is much more generic for understanding human behavior. In this perspective, the situation of Adonijah and Solomon is a case in point, as is true of David and his brothers (I Samuel 16) and others. Even when the text does not specifically mention age, the pattern obtains. Thus, Orfah is a first type, while Ruth is a second (Ruth 1:1-22), as is true of first-type Martha and second-type Mary in Luke 10:38-42. Others in the New Testament who come to mind are Andrew and Peter as well as James and John.

9. It is worthy of note that this story is generally called the parable of the prodigal son, which title is nowhere in the text. If anything, it is the parable of the elder brother, as suggested by the first two verses of Luke 15. My theory is that this designation came about since it was made by "elder brothers," who are much more likely to be running the church and ecclesiastical affairs than are "younger brothers."

10. Not all second-born children are second-type. If several years intervene, and the second sibling is of a different sex, s/he may well be a first type. Thus if there is a "good" son, and three or four years later a daughter is born, she can be a "good girl" since there is no one occupying that role. The next child, however,

whether male or female, will almost certainly be second type.

11. For a discussion of the significance of sibling position, see Walter Toman, *Family Constellation* (New York: Springer Publishing Co., 1969).

12. "Pathology elsewhere in the family . . . is reduced or eliminated by the creation of a scapegoat who carries, in effect, the pathology for the total family. Ancient lore developing around the *black sheep* has received much support (in understanding) the child who is selected to be a scapegoat." John Elderkin Bell, *Family Therapy* (New York: Jason Aronson, 1975), p. 227. See also, *inter alia,* C. Christian Beels, "The Identified Patient," *Family Therapy*, Peggy Papp, ed. (New York: Gardner Press, 1977), pp. 35 ff.; and Donald A. Block, "Including Children in Family Therapy," *Family Therapy, Theory and Practice*, Philip J. Guerin, Jr., ed. (New York: Gardner Press, 1976) pp. 168 ff.

## 5. Death and Rebirth

1. This metaphor is used by Jesus in John 3 as he converses with Nicodemus, and is picked up by Paul in such places as Rom. 6:6, Gal. 3, 4. See also, Eph. 4:22 and Col. 3:9. Unfortunately, many church people see Jesus' statement to Nicodemus as an exhortation rather than a statement of fact. Actually, the "rebirth" is not something the person can do by decision or force of will. Rather, it occurs as a response of faith to reconciling love. As we noted earlier, it is futile and cruel to say to a drowning person, "You must stay on top of the water." However true this is as a statement of fact, the tragedy is that this is precisely what the person cannot do without someone who comes to bring help.

2. We are reminded of the story of the unclean spirit and the empty house, which ends on precisely this same note (Matt. 12:43-45; Luke 11:24-26).

3. The Jacob saga is, of course, a composite of many strands and threads, woven and overlaid until gathered into the form we have today. It is beyond the scope of our discussion to sort out the various textual problems here. The basic structure is the Yahwist text, and it is to that we look primarily. Having said that, as noted

earlier, there is an underlying theological meaning in the collected data, and by seeing it whole we gain an understanding of the struggle not only of Jacob but also of ourselves and all persons. In the encounters of Bethel and Peniel followed by the meeting with Esau we are able to discover crucial clues for death and rebirth as the process of reconciliation.

4. We think of the younger son in the parable of Jesus, who gets his share of the property, and sets out for the far country (Luke 15:11-13).

5. It is ironic that the words of Laban have been called the "Mizpah Benediction." There is anything but a "benediction" in the text; rather two hostile men who realize that they cannot always be on the lookout for each other call on God to see to it that neither will cross the boundary line.

### 6. Risk and Redemption

1. The factor of "outside the wall" is suggested in various of the parables. Cf. Mark 8:23, where the blind man is healed "out of the village"; and John 20:15, when the wicked tenants of the vineyard decide that they can gain the inheritance by killing the heir. "And they cast him out of the vineyard and killed him." In like fashion, the so-called *kenosis* passage in Philippians 2 desribes the relinquishing of the security of the "walls" to seek for Adam: "though he was in the form of God, did not count equality with God a thing to be grasped, but emptied himself, taking the form of a servant, being born in the likeness of men. And being found in human form he humbled himself and became obedient unto death, even death on a cross" (vs. 6-8).

2. This point is considered in greater detail in my *Referral in Pastoral Counseling*, esp. pp. 29 ff.

# Index of Names and Subjects

Reassurance: temptation to engage in, 92. *See also* Destructive reassurance
Rebekah, 80
Rebel: behavior of, 120; Cain as, 117; characteristics of, 121; as younger sibling, 115
Rebellion, 149; in biblical narratives, 114; implications of for pastoral counseling, 157; overt, 115; as theme, 39
Rebirth, 151, 158; concept of, 180; necessity for, 178; as theme, 39
Reconciliation, 85, 123, 140, 161, 187; approach that makes possible, 208; beginning of, 148; biblical perspective on, 31; corporate nature of, 157; experience of, 29, 178; and forgiveness, 108; function of, 186; God's promise of, 38; good news of, 223; love as means for, 88; ministry of, 191; possibility for, 149; primary focus on, 41; as primary thrust of counseling, 30; process of, 40, 144, 215; through affirmation of person, 125; true, 214
Redemption: crucial dimension of, 196; in pastoral counseling, 200, 219; process of, 192; risk in, 188; as theme, 39, 193
Redemptive encounter, 138
Redemptive experience: essence of, 187; mark of, 191
Redemptive process: and biblical material, 186
*Referral in Pastoral Counseling* (Oglesby, Jr.), 12

Regularity, 181, 182
Rejection, 97; crushing blow of, 102; of minister, 198; prospect of, 91; of the self, 159
Relational dimensions: of parishioner's life, 87
Relational encounter, 42
Relationship-oriented therapy, 17
Relationships: fundamental need for, 34; primary focus on, 18, 41; risking, 150. *See also* Broken relationships
Relationship therapies, 25
Remorse: of alcoholic, 157
Repentance, 140
Resentment: language of, 86; minister's understanding of, 174; at needing help, 87
Resistance: to being found, 203; to being helped, 78; in conformist and rebel, 121; to health, 151; to loss of identity, 199; minister aware of, 175; of parishioner's ploy, 159; to pastor, 70; theme of in Bible, 152; toward relinquishing ploys, 166; to wholeness, 170
Responsibility: of the pastor, 219
Restoration, 123; of persons, 31; of real being, 105
Reward, 24
Right being, 28
Right doing, 28
Risk: crucial dimension of, 196; description of, 190; incurred by the minister, 186; in pastoral counseling, 200, 219; as theme, 39, 193
Rogers, Carl, 9

# Scriptural Index

## OLD TESTAMENT

# NEW TESTAMENT

## Scriptural Index